Int. Life

W9-CME-594

D1126774

JESUS OUR MODEL

JESUS OUR MODEL

BY

LOUIS COLIN, C.SS.R.

Translated from the French by

UNA MORRISSY

1959

HENRY REGNERY COMPANY, CHICAGO

First published in English in 1958 by the Mercier Press Limited
17 Drawbridge Street, Cork, Ireland.

Published in France under the title Jésus Notre Modèle *by Editions Saint-Paul,*
Paris.

Nihil Obstat : **JACOBUS CANONICUS BASTIBLE,**
Censor Deputatus.

IMPRIMATUR : ✠CORNELIUS,
Ep. Corcagiensis et Rossensis.

PRINTED IN THE U.S.A. BY PHOTOPRESS, INC.

CONTENTS

JESUS OUR MODEL

CHAPTER I

THE VOICE OF THE MASTER

THE idea of the imitation of Christ belongs to the sphere of revelation. Christ Himself sowed the germ of it in the Gospel, and the Church has carefully fostered and cultivated it so that in the course of the centuries it has grown like a gigantic tree sheltering all birds, that is, Christian souls, and bearing in all seasons the many and precious fruits of sanctity. Our Lord was the first teacher of imitation ; indeed who but He would have the right and authority to preach and commend it. The Gospel, therefore, is more than the voice of the Redeemer ; it is His life : the unique Ideal of perfection.

The Word became flesh in order to give the fulness of life to the world, that is supernatural life, having for its principle, its model and its final purpose God Himself. Christianity is in fact the outpouring of the life of the Most Holy Trinity over mankind. The Creation, the Incarnation, the Redemption, the founding of the Church with its priesthood and its sacraments, are all the prodigious efforts of Almighty God to raise man to Himself, to make him a participant in the divine nature, in its perfections and its holiness, to give him new life as a son of God, to make of him a being in His own likeness. It is the responsibility of the Christian soul, then, through its temporal vocation and its eternal destiny, to live like God and to resemble Him. Even the pagan philosopher Plato saw resemblance to a divine model as the ideal of human perfection.

When the Second Person of the Holy Trinity became man He recalled and defined this teaching of imitation of God which had already been promulgated in the Old Testament. "But I say to you," He taught, "love your enemies : do good to them that hate you : and pray for them that persecute and calumniate you : That you may be the children of your Father who is in heaven, who maketh his sun to rise upon the good and bad, and raineth upon the just and the

unjust . . . Be you therefore perfect, as also your heavenly
Father is perfect."[1] " Love your enemies," He went on,
" do good, and lend, hoping for nothing thereby : and your
reward shall be great, and you shall be sons of the Highest ;
for he is kind to the unthankful, and to the evil. Be ye
therefore merciful, as your Father also is merciful."[2] Here was
a teaching of unquestionable orthodoxy, in which even the
bitter logic-chopping of the Scribes and Pharisees could
find nothing to attack. Then came the moment when
Jesus manifested Himself, and claiming His title of Messiah,
declared His own Divinity. From that time He took His
rightful position as the model of sanctity for all humanity.
It is through Him henceforth that we must pass, since He
is the Way, and by imitating Him " who is the image of the
invisible God "[3] that we shall come to resemble our heavenly
Father.

Whether in hidden words or in explicit terms the doctrine
of Imitation is constantly on the lips of Christ, an essential
part of His message. "Take up my yoke upon you, and
learn of me," He taught.[4] Taking up Christ's yoke means
nothing more or less than practising, like Him and with
Him, the difficult virtues, humility, obedience, the spirit of
sacrifice. Learning of Him means understanding His teaching and putting it into practice, and in doing this becoming
more like Him, for Jesus preached only the Truth which He
also lived, and the yoke He offered He had already borne
Himself. We learn, then, from the Master, in whom word
and act are indissolubly united. He is the Master too through
the truth which He reveals and the example He urges. He *is*
the light which enlightens all our ways ; He *is* the very
virtue which He preaches : the love of the Father, the fraternal
charity which He urges, His own new commandment of
love is Himself, for He is the embodiment of all that He
utters. The most inspiring and attractive pages of the Gospel
are but fragments of His autobiography. His words are
never abstract or vague, but pour forth, realistic, luminous,

---

[1] Matth. v, 44–48.
[2] Luke. vi, 35–36.
[3] Coloss. i, 15.
[4] Matth. xi, 29.

iridescent, profound, from the very depths of His soul, which they express and reveal to us.

Christ is never the mere philosopher or rhetorician for whom virtue is no more than an appealing theme for magnificent eloquence. He is never, above all, the pharisee, whom He denounces in words of fire : " Woe to you scribes and Pharisees, hypocrites : because you are like to whited sepulchres, which outwardly appear to men beautiful, but within are full of dead men's bones, and of all filthiness."[5] And again : " The scribes and the Pharisees have sitten on the chair of Moses. All things therefore whatsoever they shall say to you, observe and do: but according to their works do ye not ; for they say and do not."[6] He Himself was the voice of truth uttering holiness, and His teaching was but the echo of His own life. When His Apostles asked : Lord, teach us to pray, His answer was to raise His eyes to heaven, and to let fall from His lips the divine prayer which all the generations of Christians throughout the ages have ceaselessly repeated : Our Father who art in heaven . . . In place of an abstract dissertation on the subject of prayer He chose an actual cry of love and adoration. However, receiving the lessons of the Master is not purely a matter of listening to His words. Much more does it mean being steeped in His spirit, His will, His soul, His whole life ; in short it consists in striving to become like Him. Though the disciple is " not above the master," yet he must use every effort to attain to His height, for what the Master is, the disciple will be.

" Following Christ " is another way of expressing the same idea, and its very simplicity conceals its wealth of meaning. " Follow me " was a familiar phrase with our Lord, and one addressed especially to His disciples, His chosen ones. " If any man will come after me, let him deny himself, and take up his cross and follow me."[7] To Saint Matthew whom He saw sitting in the custom-house He said, " Follow me." "And he arose up and followed him."[8] To the very

---

[5] Matth. xxiii, 27.
[6] Ibid. xxiii, 3.
[7] Ibid. xvi, 24.
[8] Ibid. ix, 9.

first two Apostles, Peter and Andrew, whom He saw casting a net into the sea He spoke : " Come ye after me, and I will make you to be fishers of men."[9]

It is scarcely pushing the sense of this expression too far to discern in it a hidden appeal for imitation not only exterior and material, but also interior and spiritual. Following Christ means walking in His footsteps and in the way of His soul. It means following Him along the road of His Divine Will, bathed in His light, carrying His cross, doing His work, inspired by His ideal, and pursuing with His eagerness the glory of the Father and the salvation of the world.

To the question, " What is a Christian ? " Christ replies in two words in the Gospel : " Follow me." The Christian is the man who follows Christ, not literally walking the same paths that He trod in Judea, Galilee and Samaria : nor in turning over page by page the story of the Gospels and thus recapitulating the course of our Saviour's life. The Christian follows Christ by learning from Him, by becoming His disciple, and by eventually being converted into someone whose thoughts, desires and feelings conform absolutely with those of Jesus Christ, his Master and Model.

In another phrase our Lord reiterates His " Follow me " when He utters those words weighty with depth and substance : " I am the Way, the Truth and the Life." [10] The follower of Christ must choose his route ; but his route is Christ. " I am the Way," the unique and royal way, to leave which is most certainly to go astray. It is not enough to go our Saviour's way and fit our footsteps in behind His. We must enter into Him, model ourselves on Him, even as the water poured into a vase assumed its shape. As Saint Paul puts it : " Walk ye in him,"[11] which means simply that we must advance further and further in knowledge and love and imitation of Him.

Christ is the Way, a way filled with light, " the true light, which enlighteneth every man that cometh into this world."[12]

Can we enter into this eternal and infinite glory of the God-head without ourselves absorbing something of God ? When we walk out into a beautiful, sunny day we are at once enveloped in its brightness and its light, and whoever enters into Christ, the Sun of Justice, cannot help but be invested with Him and become with Him and like Him a " child of light."[13] No one can believe in our Divine Saviour without possessing truth, and whoever possesses truth cannot but resemble Him who is Truth ; from darkness and nothingness he then becomes " light in the Lord."[14]

Christ is the Truth and the Life, the ideal, infinitely fruitful life. He embodies the supernatural life in the fulness of all its forms. He is the ideal model for the Christian, for the religious, for the priest, all of whom need only to imitate Him in order to become the perfect Christian, the perfect religious, the perfect priest.

But the Life, which is Christ, is immensely more than an ideal to contemplate and reproduce ; for it is also the very principle and source of life. We can put down our roots in Christ and from Him draw the sustenance for our own lives, so that now we live through and in Him. His Passion and Death merited this grace for us, and He has ensured that it should flow and flourish in our souls through the Holy Ghost and through the Church. Christ is the well-spring of life within us, life which overflows and fills each and every one of His spiritual children and members of His Mystical Body.

Now if we live our lives in Christ it follows that we cannot live contrary to His ways. One recognises a flower by its perfume, the source and terrain of a river from its colora-tion. Equally must the moral aspect of the true Christian recall Jesus his Model, of Whom he is but the extension and reflection. " For we are the good odour of Christ unto God," says Saint Paul.[15] Such resemblance with its obvious corollary, the imitation of Christ, finds its most vigorous and luminous expression in our Lord's discourse at the Last Supper : " Abide in me, and I in you. As the branch cannot

---

[13] I. Thess. v, 5.
[14] Eph. v, 8.
[15] II Cor. ii, 5.

bear fruit of itself, unless it abide in the vine, so neither can you, unless you abide in me. I am the vine; you the branches : he that abideth in me, and I in him, the same beareth much fruit : for without me you can do nothing."[16]

The type of perfection envisaged by our Lord, and to which with His help we aspire, is Himself, and His desire is to make every Christian soul another Christ. To collaborate with Him in this work all we have to do is to adapt ourselves to His way, as though we were but instruments in the hands of a craftsman, and to work with Him in the task of "christifying" ourselves. Infused by Christ, like the vine-shoot with the sap, we shall carry Him, as the stalk the grape, and we shall grow according to His own desire : " In this is my Father glorified ; that you bring forth very much fruit, and become my disciples."[17]

All of this, however, is only a very broad and general invitation. Let us note, then, how with words of the utmost clarity and urgency He calls upon us to observe in Him the specific virtues we should copy. He is our model in humility and self-abnegation ; the Son of God washes the feet of His apostles on His knees, and rising to His feet reminds them, "Know you what I have done to you ? You call me Master, and Lord ; and you say well, for so I am. If then I, being your Lord and Master, have washed your feet, you also ought to wash one another's feet. For I have given you an example, that as I have done to you, so you do also."[18] He is our model in devotion and sacrifice : in the face of the pretensions of the sons of Zebedee and the jealousy of the other ten He reminds them that the first duty of the master is to be humble and to serve. " He that will be first among you, shall be your servant. Even as the Son of man is not come to be ministered unto, but to minister, and to give his life a redemption for many."[19] He is our model in fraternal charity, a virtue very dear to His heart and one which He insisted was to be the distinctive mark of His followers : " A new commandment I give unto you : that you love

[16] John xv, 4-5.
[17] John xv, 8.
[18] John xiii, 15.
[19] Matth. xx, 26-28.

one another, as I have loved you, that you also love one another."[20] He is our model in patience and fortitude before persecutions : "If the world hate you, know ye, that it hath hated me before you . . . Remember my word that I said to you: The servant is not greater than his master. If they have persecuted me, they will also persecute you."[21] He is our model in obedience to His Father and obedience to the law, which He came not to abolish but to fulfil in every iota : "If you keep my commandments, you shall abide in my love ; as I also have kept my Father's commandments, and do abide in his love."[22]

In brief, and according to the authoritative voice of God Himself, if we will achieve sanctity, we must follow exactly the example of our divine Master, for as He Himself says : "The disciple is not above his master : but every one shall be perfect, if he be as his master."[23]

---

[20] John, xiii, 34.
[21] John xv, 18–20.
[22] *Ibid.* xv, 10.
[23] Luke vi, 40.

CHAPTER 2

THE TEACHING OF THE APOSTLES

THE doctrine of imitation was vigorously stressed and repeated by those faithful witnesses to the teaching of Christ, the Apostles and the Evangelists. Foremost among them was Saint Paul, from the depths of whose ardent nature pour forth appeals to follow our Lord, to put on the Lord Jesus Christ and to transform ourselves in Him. The foundation of his teaching, the aim of his apostolate, is Christ : to make Him known, to serve Him, to shed His light on souls and foster their love of Him. " My little children," he says, " of whom I am in labour again, until Christ be formed in you."[1] Walk in Jesus Christ, he tells the Colossians, draw near to Him and enter into His thoughts ; make His virtues and His feelings your own. Take root in Him like a plant in the good earth, so that you may draw from Him the life-giving grace which will make your life His. Build on Him, the corner-stone, the edifice of your sanctity, fill yourselves with Him so that His life may pervade yours and fill you to overflowing, and thus will be realised His word : " I am come that they may have life, and may have it more abundantly."[2]

Christianity is a mighty and magnificent revelation : it is the revelation of Jesus Christ in all the glory of His divinity and His humanity, of His virtues and of His life. It is the radiance of Jesus illuminating our souls with the light of His grace, until they finally reflect Him and become living portraits of Him. " But we all beholding the glory of the Lord with the open face, are transformed into the same image from glory to glory, as by the Spirit of the Lord."[3] Imitation, in Saint Paul's teaching, is simply the flower and the fruit of his doctrine of divine adoption and incorporation in Christ.

---

[1] Gal. iv, 19.
[2] John x, 10.
[3] II Cor. iii, 18.

The Word was made flesh to redeem us and to communicate to us the grace of divine adoption. By this means we are born of God, children of our heavenly Father, brethren of Jesus Christ, and, says Saint Paul, " because you are sons, God hath sent the Spirit of his Son into your hearts, crying : Abba, Father."[4]   Our Lord and the Christian soul are thus two brethren having the same Father, living the same divine life, and enjoying the same destiny and the same inheritance. It is not too much to hope that the same infinite and eternal love may envelop both of them.

Between Christ and the Christian soul, however, there exists more than a fraternal link ; it is in reality an incorporation.   As Christians we enter into Christ and become something of Him ; thus absorbed in His divine personality we are identified with Him. We live in Christ and of Christ as the infant in the womb which derives life from its mother, and we become a mystical extension of His person and His holiness.   We are one body of which He is the head and we the members, animated by one spirit and living one life. If we are thus one with Him we certainly cannot think or love or will other than He does, and so perfect imitation, according to Saint Paul, is simply the logical consequence of his teaching of the Mystical Body of Christ.

The Christ offered as our Model by Saint Paul is Christ in His fulness : the God-Man with His infinite perfections and His human virtues. It is the Son in the bosom of the Father, and it is too the Word Incarnate suffering, dying, laid in the tomb, risen glorious. It is the historic Christ and also the mystical Christ, in Whom all is wonderful and imitable.

What Saint Paul loves to concentrate upon, the particular and novel aspect of his teaching, is the whole Christ rather than certain features of Him. Without neglecting what might be called the smaller occurrences, he leans towards the central and cardinal events of His life : His Incarnation, Crucifixion, Death, Burial, Resurrection and Ascension. These are the mysteries which should be spiritually reproduced in the Christian soul turning it towards Christ. The broad canvas rather than the miniature attracts and inspires his genius.

---

[4] Gal. iv, 6.

He lingers little on the accidental, this action or that attitude, that saying of Christ, but goes straight to the essential, to the principal action. His life of Jesus consequently is neither anecdotal nor episodic but is mystical rather than historical. The historical figure of the Redeemer which appears in his Epistles is just a lightning sketch, and the character of his exhortations to imitate Him are more or less general. For example he tells the Colossians, " All whatsoever you do in word or in work, do all in the name of the Lord Jesus Christ " : [5] Again in order to stimulate the Corinthians to generosity towards the poor of Jerusalem he urges : " For you know the grace of our Lord Jesus Christ, that being rich he became poor for your sakes ; that through his poverty you might be rich."[6]

But the Divinity, the soul of our Lord ; this was what delighted Saint Paul, this was what enkindled the flame of his love and this was what he urged us to imitate. The life of Christ, like all human lives, was both public and private. His exterior and public life consisted of innumerable words, actions, situations ; an enormous collection of occupations, labours, prayers, struggles and sufferings. His interior life, however, the source of the former, opened out in the sanctuary of His own conscience and was a whole world in itself of thoughts, desires, affections, of wishes and virtues, and of relationships, permanent or passing but always ineffable, with the Most Holy Trinity.

Accordingly the Pauline teaching of the imitation of Christ has for its supreme object the intimate life of our Lord : the reproduction of His interior rather than of His exterior life in the soul. In place of mere mimicry which would result in the most superficial of resemblances, Saint Paul's teaching is that the imitation of the interior life of Christ must begin by a profound assimilation in and transformation into Him. After all, it matters very little whether a child resembles his father in figure or voice so long as he inherits his spirit and intelligence, his nobility of character and his various virtues. So the essential for the Christian, as Saint Paul says, is to have the " mind of Christ," so as to

---

[5] Coloss. iii, 17.
[6] II Cor. viii, 9.

be able to see and value all things in His divine and infallible way. It is essential to watch over and preserve this outlook in ourselves, the mind of the " true light, which enlighteneth every man that cometh into this world " so that we may draw from it the full and pure truth, and live it, and shed its radiance around us. To have the " mind of Christ " is to participate in all His " treasures of wisdom and knowledge," [7] and in the light of His Spirit, and to possess the fulness of faith in preparation for our enjoyment of the Beatific Vision.

" For let this mind be in you, which was also in Christ Jesus," [8] says Saint Paul to the Philippians. Let us look for a moment at the mind which he urges to imitate. Here are the infinite depths of humility, adoration and love for His heavenly Father ; the boundless pity and universal forgiveness for mankind ; the tenderness for His mother and loyalty to His friends ; the heroic sanctity, generosity, compassion ; the charity which poured from Him continuously from the cradle through the Cross to the altar. Saint Paul's familiar expression, synonomous of course with perfect imitation, and one which conveys his meaning precisely is : " Put ye on the Lord Jesus Christ." " For as many of you as have been baptised in Christ, have put on Christ," [9] he tells the Galatians, and to the Romans he urges, " But put ye on the Lord Jesus Christ, and make not provision for the flesh in its concupiscences." [10] Imitation of Christ, clearly, is not to be, like a work of art, merely the creation of a likeness, but a complete immersion in Christ, a new way of life, of which Christ is the principle, the ideal and the end. Our baptism, teaches Saint Paul, plunges us into Christ, so that we have become " christified."

The final aspect of the soul of Christ which is expounded in Saint Paul's Doctrine, is His spirit of sacrifice. " O senseless Galatians," he cries, " who hath bewitched you that you should not obey the truth, before whose eyes Jesus Christ hath been set forth, crucified among you ? " [11] Life is an

---

[7] Coloss. ii, 3.
[8] Phil. ii, 5.
[9] Gal. iii, 27.
[10] Rom. iii, 14.
[11] Gal. iii, 1

arena where the Christian soul fights with his eyes fixed on
his Saviour, who Himself " having joy set before him,
endured the cross, despising the shame."[12]   Therefore, if
we would follow Christ we cannot refuse to fight and
perhaps to die ; or to walk where Christ has already passed.

Saint Paul accomplished first in himself the imitation
of Christ crucified. As he wrote to the Galatians : " I
bear the marks of the Lord Jesus in my body,"[13] and again :
" with Christ I am nailed to the cross."[14]   He was no mere
theorist on the subject of imitation of Christ, but a glorious
and incomparable practitioner.   Perhaps no one else, except
our Blessed Lady, has presented such a magnificent example
of the mystical reproduction of the Redeemer. He knew
that himself, and unhesitatingly, though completely without
pride, he offered himself as a model to the new Christians
whom he taught.   " Be ye followers of me, as I also am of
Christ."[15] To the Thessalonians he wrote : " For yourselves know how you ought to imitate us."[16]   From that
dramatic moment when on the road to Damascus Christ
revealed Himself to His persecutor Paul had one thought
and one passion only, Christ. At one stroke he was transformed and from thence sought only to love and to preach
Christ, to extend His kingdom and to engender Him in
souls. To this end he dedicated in the midst of the terrible
persecution and unto death all his immense energies. In
this soul indeed Christ entered and conquered. And His
tremendous and triumphal entry stimulated in the Apostle
such a complete sublimation of his own human personality
that it seemed to give place altogether to that of Jesus Christ,
so that he could write in all simple truth : " And I live,
now not I, but Christ liveth in me."[17]

Saint Paul is the pre-eminent teacher of imitation of Christ
but he is not the only one. Accompanying him are to be
heard many voices in the early Church transmitting faithfully the teaching of the Master.

---

[12] Heb. xii, 2.
[13] Gal. vi, 17.
[14] Gal. ii, 19.
[15] I Cor. xi, 1.
[16] II Thess. iii, 7.
[17] Gal. II, 20.

After recalling that perfect charity consists in keeping the word of God, and that thus we shall know if indeed we are " in Him " Saint John goes on to say : " He that saith he abideth in him, ought himself also to walk, even as he walked."[18]

Saint Peter also, wishing to console sorrowful souls, recalled to them the example of the Redeemer, and urged them not to forget that " Christ also suffered for us, leaving you an example that you should follow his steps."[19] He reminds all Christians that if it should be necessary to suffer persecution for justice' sake this would be a glorious and blessed opportunity for increasing resemblance to Jesus Christ, who " also died once for our sins, the just for the unjust,"[20] and he observes that " it is better doing well (if such be the will of God) to suffer, than doing ill."[21] " But if you partake of the sufferings of Christ," he goes on " rejoice that when his glory shall be revealed, you may also be glad with exceeding joy."[22]

Such is the triumph of the imitation of Christ crucified, which here below should be to us a source of divine joy, and will merit " for us above measure exceedingly an eternal weight of glory."[23]

---

[18] I Ep. John. ii, 6.
[19] I Pet. ii, 21.
[20] *Ibid.* iii, 18.
[21] *Ibid.* iii, 17.
[22] *Ibid.* iv, 13.
[23] II Cor. iv, 17.

CHAPTER 3

THE LIFE OF THE CHURCH

CHRISTIANITY is a way of life, both individual and collective. "I am come," said our Lord, "that they may have life."[1] This supernatural life puts down its roots and grows and develops first of all in each individual soul. Primarily and essentially religion is a personal virtue, and the kingdom of God is in ourselves.

But to the Christian religion which He founded our Lord has given the structure of a proper society, a visible universal society with a head, members, legislation, functions and a very special purpose. It is a society possessing a name, the Catholic Church, and living its own public and official life, of which the liturgy is one of the principal outward manifestations.

The Church being a hierarchical organisation includes all the states of life within her boundaries, and amongst these the religious state has pride of place. For all the states of life, however, which subsist within the Church the imitation of Christ is at once the ideal to be attained and the source of inspiration and attainment.

The first Christians lived their lives in the direct radiance of the Redeemer, within the warm glow of His teaching and of His love. Christ Himself in a sense *was* their religion. That is to say they found in Him, by precept and by practice, their ideal of perfection in accordance with their faith and the hope of their salvation. In those days the true Christian was oriented and concentrated almost exclusively on the person of Jesus ; not like our modern times when the Church is enriched almost to the point of luxury, even of encumbrance, with a mass of devotions. To live a truly religious life meant in effect but to know, to love and to imitate Christ. The very origin of the word "Christian" derived from that conception : the man who professed to be a follower of Jesus Christ was simply a Christian. There was nothing

[1] John, x, 10.

abstract or hazy about this religion, whose dogma and philosophy were embodied in the veneration of the Redeemer. "Jesus," says Saint Polycarp, "is ceaselessly offered to the faithful as the model for the Christian and the ideal of holiness." The teaching of a long line of bishops and doctors simply extended and amplified this doctrine, which was what Saint Paul had already taught.

Then came the persecutions. Now more than ever the Christians felt the need while contemplating Christ of leaning on Him. Before the face of the Crucified who died for love of man the agony of the martyrs became an ecstasy and their death a triumph. "Blessed are they who suffer persecution for justice' sake for theirs is the kingdom of heaven."[2] To suffer with Christ, for Christ and like Christ, was a divine blessing and a prelude to paradise. Saint Ignatius of Antioch in a letter to the Romans brimming with joy and the power of grace writes, " Let me be thrown to the lions and the bears : it is the shortest road to heaven . . . allow me to become in some sort an imitator of Christ, dying for men . . . " Saint Polycarp standing before the stake uttered in union with Christ his supreme sacerdotal prayer : " I bless you, God, I who am the least of your servants and give you thanks that you have considered me worthy to suffer for you . . . what a great honour to be able to put to my lips the chalice from which your Son, Jesus Christ, so willingly drank."

The ensuing generations continue, with alternation of greater or lesser fervour, in winter somnolence and in spring-like ardour, to love and to carry out this imitation of Christ. Like all dogmas it too develops and grows. Throughout the centuries it has been defined and extended to appeal to all men as a practical method of sanctification. At the present time we are seeing this doctrine enjoy a renewal of general favour, not only among the theologians and ascetics, but among the main body of the faithful. More and more Christian souls are becoming conscious of their incorporation with Christ and savouring the result : the blossoming within themselves of the life of Christ. Even more than the Chris-

[2] Matt. v, 10.

tian life in the world the monastic life seems also to be enjoying this flowering of the teaching of imitation. For the religious of contemporary life just as for the monk of ancient times Christ is still the ideal to contemplate and to copy.

Nudum sequi Christum nudum : naked, to follow the naked Christ expressed in brief the lives of the fathers of the desert. The same Christocentric ideal permeated the legislation of the monastic orders ; among them all is to be found the same aspiration : to reproduce Christ in themselves ; to live His life. " For the love of Christ "was the phrase dearest to Saint Benedict ; if the loving presence of Jesus had not enlightened him the cloister would have appeared nothing but a prison. Then as the Orders and Congregations increased, the idea of the imitation of Christ inspired and penetrated their rule ever more deeply.

We find imitation, too, to be the keynote of the liturgy. The liturgy, as has been wisely said, is at one and the same time learning, art and life. Learning : of which such a large proportion is the loving discovery of the Redeemer. Art : its masterpiece being the mystical reproduction of Christ in souls. Life : the life of Christ flowing as the life-blood of an organism through the whole Church and each and every one of its members. To live a liturgical life would be to live Jesus Christ Himself, and to transform one's whole religious outlook by the practice of imitation. In fact, when we consider the object, ministry and purpose of the Catholic religion we can perceive that it is a religion permeated with a God to contemplate, to glorify, to pray to and to reproduce in our own lives.

In the liturgy the Redeemer occupies a special place at its very centre. Without forgetting the Father and the Holy Ghost, whom she adores, and the Blessed Virgin and the Saints whom she venerates, the Church has always given to the Word Incarnate a special devotion. In the holy sacrifice of the Mass, in the Divine Office, and in the prayers of the ritual, how frequently our Lord appears, as an historical or as a mystical figure, in sorrow and in triumph. There are revealed to us the ancient and ever new mysteries of His temporal and His eternal life, and they are dwelt upon, not merely to jog the memories of the more lukewarm faithful, but as a direct appeal to the mind, the heart and the will ; to call us to a more profound and loving knowledge of Christ, that we may the more perfectly follow Him and the more ineffably become one with Him. The cycle of the liturgy brings us the life of Christ in all its variety of aspects and multiplicity of actions and works for our daily contemplation and imitation.

The living Incarnation of religion, Jesus bears in His own soul the whole of Christian worship, of which He is the first, the universal and the unique minister. The Church, the priests and the laity, are in reality only the servants of the Sovereign Priest, and could not of themselves perform a public act of worship were it not for His mandate and the manner in which they are united to Him. All who want not merely to assist at but to participate in the sacrifice of the Mass, in the ceremonies and the prayers of the liturgy, must first enter into Christ, must become one through Him and with Him and in Him, and in one sublime oblation, together with the Son, offer to the Father the adoration, the entreaties, the expiation and the thanksgiving of the Church. This is nothing more or less than again and with greater merit to imitate Christ in the accomplishment of His priestly functions.

The glorification of the Most Holy Trinity is the supreme purpose of the Christian worship, but it is not the only one. In the mind of the Church the liturgy is also an inexhaustible source of sanctity and the inner life of the soul of Christians. The interior life consists in participating ever more abundantly in the life of Christ. To fill the soul with devotion to the spirit of the liturgy is to approach with continuously lengthening steps towards Him who is the ideal of perfection. In the prayers of the liturgy there are innumerable texts which bring this holy imitation of Christ to mind and implore it as a special grace.

From her origin then until our own day the Catholic Church through her worship has lived thus the life of Jesus, allowing the teachings of the Son of God to come to fruition in her liturgy.

CHAPTER 4

THE ECHO OF THE CENTURIES

BESIDES being the leaven of the spiritual life the imitation of Christ is a doctrine; and it was a doctrine even before its vivifying power could be assayed. It is incorporated in the body of Catholic dogma and shines as one of the brightest jewels in that glittering collection of revealed truths.

We have considered already the precepts of Jesus Christ and His Apostles relating to imitation, yet these were but the introduction to the doctrine uttered in the very dawn of the Christian day. Throughout the course of all the centuries the Church has studied the succinct teaching of the divine Master, and plumbing its profundities has continued to spread it, using the powerful voices of her doctors and her schools, her ascetic and mystical theologians, to make it echo and reverberate through the spiritual world. Let us listen for a short while to some of the echoes of this two-thousand-year-old tradition.

First of all there are the Fathers of the Church, incomparable commentators on the Holy Scripture. From the limitless field of patristic writing there is borne the fragrant litany of the holy virtues of our Saviour : humility, chastity, patience, firmness, obedience, prayerfulness, self-abnegation, poverty, zeal, benignity, mercy, charity. Among the most eloquent and authentic representatives of the tradition Saint Augustine holds an important, if not indeed the first, place. He acts both as a source and as a starting point, since he recapitulates all the teaching which has gone before him, while at the same time he opens up for the future new avenues of thought which ever since have been assiduously frequented.

The dogma of our incorporation in Christ is in particular very familiar to him, and no one, perhaps, before his time has understood so well how to plumb its depths or how to exploit its usefulness in helping us to imitate Him. To know, to love, to imitate Jesus Christ in order that He may live and grow in our souls is the essential element of Augustinian spirituality.

The same doctrine is stressed in the writings of the Greek Fathers, in particular those of Saint Gregory Nazianzen and Saint John Chrysostom. When we come down the centuries to Saint Bernard we see how his earnest contemplation and his passionate love for our Saviour find their expression in the imitation of the God made Man ; and their fulfilment in absolute conformity with the Word of God. " Asceticism," he says, " becomes before everything else an asceticism of conformity with the mysteries of the earthly life of our Redeemer."

The doctrine of imitation is found in the majority of the great schools of spiritual thought, of which here we need only to cite two very important representatives, the Ignatian and the Bérullian.

Ignatian spirituality is completely expressed in the *Exercises,* and has always derived from that source. Actually the *Exercises* are nothing more nor less than a methodical and wonderfully effective plan for the imitation of Christ. The last three weeks are consecrated wholly to meditation on Jesus Christ, to the contemplation of His birth, life and death, His resurrection and His ascension ; a loving and fertile contemplation, which through the practice of His virtues and the assimilation of His holiness results in the reproduction of the Redeemer in the soul.

The ideal of the retreatant making the Exercises could be said to be the realisation in his own person of the dictum of Saint Augustine : "We are all in Christ, and of Christ, and we are Christ." The determining motive which Saint Ignatius uses to convince the soul, to strengthen it in the face of sacrifice and to support it in difficult and heroic decisions, is none other than the perfect imitation of our Lord. Jesus did it : very well then, I shall do it. Jesus is the model for us to copy, the king to serve, the leader to follow so that we may conquer the world and give the maximum glory to God.

For Saint Ignatius the imitation of Jesus Christ is an ascetical way ; it is a conflict which requires the spirit of sacrifice and the death of self, where the will is called upon to play a stern but, in co-operation with grace, a victorious role. The *Exercises* in a word are a storehouse of moral strength in the work of imitation.

The commentators upon them, and they have been many, have never sought to twist or soften their text. Despite certain little " family " disagreements, his sons have jealously guarded the original purity of thought of their holy Founder. In the Company of Jesus the cult of the Incarnate Word remains traditional ; and Ignatian spirituality continues to be a brilliant illustration of Saint Paul's text : " I live, now not I, but Christ liveth in me."

That certain cautious ascetics in their study of Saint Paul have placed the accent on the " now not I " while other more adventurous mystics have attached their preference to the " Christ liveth in me " does not really matter. What is indisputable is that in the long succession of spiritual writers, the majority and these the most distinguished have given first place in their works to the doctrine of love and imitation of Christ.

Of all the schools of spiritual thought none has placed greater emphasis on the doctrine of the imitation than that of the French spiritual writers of whom the most illustrious representatives are Bérulle, Condren, Olier, Saint Vincent de Paul, Saint John Eudes. Christ is truly the centre of their teaching. Everything derives from that and returns to it. The Christian life, priestly holiness, universal sanctification can be summed up in the contemplation of Jesus Christ, in loving and in imitating Him.

To be united with Christ, they teach, it is essential to divest oneself of all that might prove obstructive to such a union. Whoever wishes to be filled with Christ must first be emptied of self, for it is impossible without renouncing one's personal life to live the life of the Redeemer. Self-abnegation in order to follow Christ is the sum of Christianity and their *abneget semetipsum* is uttered with a force almost approaching violence. We must detach ourselves from all created things that we may cling only to Christ ; relinquish ourselves entirely that we may embrace Christ completely ; strive after annihilation of our proud and sensual natures to the point where we become nothing at all except in God and for

God. Vitiated by original sin our nature needs to be cleansed of its vices and purified of its weaknesses ; the struggle is between the flesh and the spirit ; the old man must disappear to make room for the new.

Once this self-annihilation is accomplished, the valleys filled in, as it were, and the mountains levelled, the way is open for the coming of Jesus. Oneness with Christ is achieved by participation in His mysteries, that is the actions, events and sufferings which are the warp and weft of His mortal, eucharistic and heavenly life. They dwell on the importance of distinguishing between the mysteries of the body and the spirit, the transitory and the permanent. His birth in Bethlehem, His flight into Egypt, His presentation in the Temple, His manual labour in Nazareth, His baptism in the Jordan, the curing of the lepers and the blind, the agony of Gethsemani, the institution of the Holy Eucharist, the crucifixion between two thieves : all these are the happenings of a day or of an hour, measured by time and completed in history.

The inner sentiments, however, of the Heart of Jesus, which were the inspiration and the mainspring of His sacred life : self-annihilation, abandonment, adoration, holiness, reparation, compassion, generosity, love, zeal, these divine realities are not completed at all. Now, after the passage of centuries, they remain as vital a part in the immortal soul of Christ as at the beginning. So it is as we know with ourselves that certain joys and sorrows survive the causes which engendered them. The soul of Jesus remains thus for ever the spiritual sanctuary of the mysteries of His earthly and heavenly existence. Imitation of Him consists, therefore, in penetrating this sanctuary and appropriating these mysteries, extracting from each in turn by contemplation, love and prayer, the grace, the virtue and the spirit peculiar to it. Reliving the mysteries of Christ in ourselves we make the Christian life an extension of the Incarnation, and of the works, sufferings and triumphs of the Redeemer.

A special merit of the French school of thought in this matter was the basing of its teaching on a solid dogmatic and traditional foundation : the Mystical Body, and our incorporation in Christ. Not that either before or after the French mystics anyone had misrepresented or forgotten the teaching of Saint Paul. Nevertheless it is helpful to see there, plainly indicated, the source from which these inspiring and beautiful lessons are drawn.

It remains only to reiterate that this has been Catholic teaching throughout the ages. The mere listing of the authors, the books and the articles which either *ex professo* or in suitable context treat of the doctrine of the imitation of Christ would by itself make up a huge bibliography.

CHAPTER 5

THE IDEAL FOR THE CHRISTIAN

THE moral doctrine of the imitation of Jesus Christ as revealed by Sacred Scripture, handed down by tradition and lived by the Church is deeply rooted in theology, and its rational origin is the secret of its duration and fertility. We imitate Christ because He is the ideal of all perfection, human and divine. As the Word of God He is the supreme example for all creation. Nothing created whether spiritual or material is more than a reflection of His beauty and the merest vestige of His Essence.

As the genius of the artist is recognised by the quality of his greatest work, so too for anyone who has eyes to see nature can be a revelation of God. The uncluttered vision of the saints knew how to discover and admire the power of the Creator in the immensity of the oceans, His wisdom in the inscrutable stars, His infinite love among the flowers of the field. All that is speaks of God and reflects Him, because everything bears the mark of His hand and the sign of His heart. Yet that which in the physical world was merely a cloudy image of God became in the world of man a luminous reflection. "Let us make man," said Jehovah, "in our image,"[1] and breathing on the model of clay God imprinted upon it the likeness of His Word. Humanity thus carved in the pattern of the Divinity was wakened unto life as a living mirror reflecting the Most Holy Trinity.

Thus Adam, the miniature of God, had only to maintain the original splendour of the marvellous portrait that he was and by the innocence of his life and his love for his Creator to reflect His characteristics. Unfortunately Adam failed and thwarted this royal programme of imitation. He sinned, and his sin was really a tentative, albeit abortive, attempt at sacrilegious imitation. "You shall be as Gods," was the satanic suggestion which had of course to culminate in dread degradation. The favoured child of God was now

[1] Gen. i, 26.

23

no more than a man, a poor lamentable object of whom the Lord spoke ironically : "Behold Adam is become as one of us . . . "[2]

Yet the divine Craftsman did not forget His masterpiece. He took this fallen broken creature into His hands again and started to remould and re-make him more beautiful than before the Fall. But now it was necessary for man to struggle for his salvation, and so for this purpose God put before men's eyes His Incarnate Word as a visible and tangible model, within the reach of all. This was one of the motives of the Incarnation ; by making the imitation of Christ easy, to make universal the imitation of God. In other words God gave to man a second chance : first He created man and He now became man, that in Him man might become God.

From henceforth men had before their eyes an ideal to contemplate : our Lord Himself, His person and His life, His qualities and His mysteries, His actions, His sufferings and His virtues. He is an ideal at once sublime and popular since He was both human and divine ; and He is a universal ideal, since there is nothing of truth, beauty, goodness or holiness which does not take its source from the eminent bounty of Christ.

Jesus is the prototype of humanity, of man such as God conceived from all eternity. He is the realisation of the human ideal : the most beautiful of the children of men, if it be true that beauty is composed of integrity, harmony and splendour. He is the perfect man in every way. There is no flaw in Him, neither in His essence nor in His faculties, in His virtues nor in His works. In Him all is excellent. There is no lack, no moral twist, no physical blemish. He is a being in no way defective or incomplete, He who in His transcendental totality possesses human nature.

In this Man-God harmony is all. Sin had warped Adam's nature, made man a creature of imbalance in conflict with himself and in opposition to God. Christ who was entrusted with the restoration of balance becomes the example of fundamental and primary order. He is the harmonious and peaceful Being in whom is nothing of discord or of

---

[2] Gen. iii, 22.

evil. Jesus lived in the centre of a serenity which was simply
a reflection of the peace of heaven. His lower human faculties are quietly controlled and subjected to the absolute
dominion of His will, which in its turn is oriented towards
His Father and immutably fixed in His divine will. Christ
is the absolute master of Himself, the loving servant of the
Father, the epitome of moral order.

His luminous intelligence perceives without shadow or
obscurity the purest and highest forms of truth : knowledge,
prudence, wisdom. His heart, which in company with the
joyous Saint Paul we can contemplate and adore, is suffused
with tenderness and strength, with delicacy and heroism,
with love and generosity, with enthusiasm and mercy. His
will, the sanctuary of all the moral virtues, is loyal and vigorous to a supreme degree. His integrity is absolute and
indomitable ; on the road of duty which led Him bleeding
and agonised to the ignominious death of the cross, nothing
halted or diverted Him. His was an incorruptible conscience
which never knew the slightest fall or shadow of weakness.
" Which of you shall convince me of sin ? " He asked. And
no one could.

Jesus is the model of all mankind and especially of the
Christian. The Christian is a God-fearing person, coming
from God, living in Him, confessing Him and returning to
Him, and of this *modus vivendi* Jesus is the supreme
example.

Christianity by its nature, origin and purpose is a system
of worship which by forging spiritual links and defining
sacred duties binds the practising Christian to God his Creator.
The duties of adoration, thanksgiving and expiation, the
necessity for prayer and sacrifice are generated by the Christian
faith and matured by Christian charity, and all are exemplified
in the soul of the Redeemer.

Christ Himself, in founding the Christian religion became
the soul, the living, palpable and eternal expression of it.
If He were alone upon this earth Christianity would nevertheless exist in His integrity and His splendour. The Incarnate Word is the religion, the personal link which unites
God and men, and it is He, the leader and representative of
men, who henceforth renders to God the worship which is

His due.   The religious, the Christian, can be nothing at all
but with Christ and in Christ, their model.

Jesus our model . . . and our brother.   By an ineffable
process, independent of flesh and blood, we are born of God
even as Jesus Christ, and our baptism in the Holy Ghost,
an actual spiritual rebirth, makes us children of the Father.
At one stroke, then, all religion is transformed, binding
man to God by links essentially supernatural and filial.   The
veneration of the servant is transmuted into the devotion of
the son and when we adore, praise, entreat or love God
it is always with Jesus our model and our brother that we
say, " Our Father who art in heaven."

Born of God who has bestowed upon us something of His
divine nature, we partake easily and rightfully in the life of
the Trinity : for that is precisely the Christian life, an ineffable
participation in the life of God.   It is the life which is called
sanctifying grace, upon which, as upon the branches of a
tree, there begin to blossom the infused virtues and gifts
of the Holy Ghost.   It is the life whose fulness and source
are to be found in Christ.   " I am the Life."[3]

The Christian is in addition the temple of the Holy Trinity.
" If anyone love me, he will keep my word, and my Father
will love him, and we will come to him, and will make our
abode with him."[4]   We are inclined to imagine the presence
of God in us somewhat in the manner of the host in the
ciborium, but it is not in the least like that.   God's presence
in man is an indwelling, a union, which gives rise to personal
rapports, to intimate and delightful exchanges of thought
and feeling between the soul and Him, such as faith, self-
abandonment, love, prayer on the one side, and tenderness,
goodness, forgiveness, abundance of graces and blessings
on the other.   The secret of such an interior life, of which
Christ provides the incomparable example, lies in our having
the same awareness of our relationship with the Father that
He had, and in sustaining and developing it.

The inner life of Christ is the model for the inner life of
our own souls which one day will enter upon life eternal.
As we came from God so we shall return to Him ; here on

---

[3] John xi, 25.
[4] John xiv, 23.

earth we are merely travellers without a permanent home. We journey on, weary fighters, hope in our hearts and our eyes on our heavenly home ; waiting only for our *nunc dimittis* to attain the family dwelling and enjoying peace everlasting. Yet while we remain here Jesus is the master we must follow. From heaven where He has gone before us He shows us in Himself what we shall be, and at the same time indicates to us the road to take if we will join Him and partake of our inheritance from the Father.

To sum up, if we wish to be and to live as Christians all we need to do is to imitate Jesus Christ, to realise that we are sons of the Father, brothers of Christ, to enter more and more into the state of filial piety towards the Father, to ensure in ourselves to the point of sanctity the development of sanctifying grace with its virtues and its gifts, to maintain active and permanent contact between our souls and the Holy Trinity in us, and so, in the company of our great Friend to travel surely and joyously towards eternal beatitude.

CHAPTER 6

JESUS, RELIGIOUS AND PRIEST

CHRIST is religion, living and eternal. It is not surprising, therefore, to discover in Him the model for the Christian and also for the religious and the priest. Let us consider the religious life, for a moment, from the following aspects : its basis, devotion of oneself to the service of God ; its essential elements are poverty, chastity, obedience ; its framework is the holy Rule ; its different forms are the contemplative life, the active life, and the life combining both. Finally, it has a double purpose, personal sanctity and the apostolate of souls. We observe immediately that Christ embodies in His Person the ideal of the religious, and perfection in this state cannot but consist in the imitation of Him.

The religious state in the final analysis is the oblation of a soul and the consecration of a life in the service of God. To enter into the service of God is the classical description of it which falls naturally from the pen of the spiritual writer. " The monastery is a school for the service of God," says Saint Benedict. The monk lives no longer for himself but for God ; he belongs no longer to himself but to God. His religious profession is an act of surrender total and irrevocable. Cut off from the world he must be, if not by means of the cloister and the grille, at least in spirit and in heart. Even in the midst of the world, which he cannot always avoid, he is not of the world by thought, feeling or act. He lives apart, withdrawn from the masses, specially consecrated to the worship of God.

Obviously by this standard our Lord was a religious from the moment of His Incarnation. The human nature assumed by the Word became the absolute and inalienable property of God. He kept nothing back, but surrendered body and soul, powers and faculties, to God and to the service of God. " The Son of Man is come not to be served but to serve " :[1]

---

[1] Matt. xx, 28.

to serve His brethren and above all His Father. In fact, the entire life of our Redeemer was one immense service rendered to God and to humanity. The first servant of the Father, He is by that the first religious and of all religious the most detached and the holiest.

Note how from time to time He indicated His unchanging opposition to the spirit of the world. " The world knew him not."[2] " If the world hate you, know ye, that it hath hated me before you."[3] Nothing in His teaching or His life suggests or recalls the world or bridges the gulf that existed between Him and it.

Jesus, model of religious, wore all His life the royal livery of poverty, chastity and obedience. From the destitution of the stable to the nakedness of the cross, our Saviour devotedly loved and heroically practised poverty. He espoused it in life, and in its embraces He chose to die.

His chastity was a virginity of heart and soul ; a spotless purity whose fragrance has enraptured and held captive countless souls.

Obedience, above all, was the virtue of His choice. The first thirty years of His life are summed up in the words, " He was subject to them," and He concluded that life by His death on the cross in obedience to the will of the Father. The religious state has to be understood as a Rule of life which by its framework and spirit is designed to serve God. Christ the religious also had His Rule—a Rule that had been laid down for Him by the prophets who foretold the life of the coming Messiah ; a Rule that was held constantly before Him by the Holy Spirit, the voice of the Father. With loving precision our Lord lived out this Rule in the letter and the spirit to the last day of His life on earth, doing nothing but what was the will of His Father.

There are no aspects of the religious life which the Word Incarnate has not known and Himself experienced. Nazareth in its obscurity, its silence, its labour and its hidden prayer typifies the contemplative life, a life which He has continued for twenty centuries in the tabernacle. After Nazareth came His active life in Judea and Galilee, with its preaching, healing,

---

[2] John i, 10.
[3] John xv, 18.

hardships and sufferings, which has set the ideal of the missionary apostle of preaching, instructing and charitable works. Yet at all times, let it be remembered that His active life was called forth and sustained by a spirit of continual prayer and burning love. Always with Him action was the outward manifestation of an interior life of contemplation and prayer ; His whole life in its perfect and harmonious blending of the active and the contemplative is the complete ideal of the religious state. In short, considering the religious life from the viewpoint of its two-fold purpose of personal sanctification and the salvation of souls, the life of Christ was that of the perfect monk.

Personal sanctity before all : the striving for perfection generously pursued day by day is the first and fundamental duty of the religious for one fulfils one's vocation only in so far as one labours to achieve personal sanctification.

We come now to a discussion of Christ, the ideal of the priesthood.

We priests shall never understand what we are or what we ought to be unless we hold constantly before us the image of the eternal High Priest. He has revealed to us the dignity of our priestly calling together with the powers and functions it confers and the virtues it demands.

Of his nature the priest is a mediator. Set apart, placed between God and man, the priest is the living link which unites the one with the other ; he is a human bridge spanning heaven and earth, along which flow the commands, the blessings and the graces from above, and the worship, prayers and petitions from below. Now our Lord Jesus Christ is the supreme Mediator. " He is the mediator of the new testament,"[4] says Saint Paul, and again, " For there is one God, and one mediator of God and men, the man Christ Jesus."[5] What is even more, He is not only a priest but the very priesthood itself, the living principle and source of our sacerdotal life, as He is wisdom, power and goodness.

The sacerdotal character in Christ is not, as it is in us, something deliberately created and extrinsic, but is of the very essence of the Man-God. Jesus Christ is a priest by

---
[4] 1 Heb. ix, 15.
[5] I Tim. ii, 5.

reason of His Incarnation, which in effect was His consecration. The Word by taking flesh vivified, elevated and made divine the humanity which He assumed, and by that act marked it with the sacerdotal seal.

It was in the most pure womb of the Blessed Virgin Mary that the ordination of Jesus as priest took place and the Consecrator was the Holy Spirit Himself. At that ineffable moment when Mary conceived Jesus the priest, she brought into existence the Catholic priesthood and became the mother of all priests.

Christ the priest and mediator works unceasingly for the glory of God and the salvation of men. His first function in the name of the humanity which He represented was to glorify the Father by adoration and thanksgiving, atonement and prayer, obedience, trust and love. This was His unique mission during His time on earth, is still so in heaven. He lived only for the interests of the Father, " I live by the Father,"[6] so that His sacerdotal life was, is and will always be an infinite glorification of the Most Holy Trinity.

Our Saviour glorified God and, the second function of the priest, He redeemed and saved the world. It was for our salvation that the Word took flesh and became a priest . . . *Et propter nostram salutem descendit de coelis, et incarnatus est.* The priesthood is a service and our Lord, the model for all priests, gave His life in that service for the redemption of mankind. Jesus the priest was the first servant of men. He loved all men with a burning zeal which knew no limits ; for them He was ready to spend Himself even to the laying down of His life. When He left this earth He did not leave them orphaned, but provided them with His Church, His sacraments and the Holy Ghost. Thus to every man, without exception, Christ the priest continues to offer salvation, faith which illumines, hope which sustains, pardon which releases, strength which triumphs over evil, and above all love . . . charity, the principle and pledge of eternal life. " We adore Thee O Christ, and we praise Thee, because by Thy holy cross Thou hast redeemed the world."

Christ was enabled to fulfil His double function of glorifying God and redeeming mankind because of His infinite holiness.

---

[6] John vi, 58.

Both Sacred Scripture and tradition demand sanctity in a high degree from the priest ; sanctity composed of purity, the spirit of sacrifice and love. In Jesus we have the sovereign priest. " For it was fitting that we should have such a high priest, holy, innocent, undefiled, separated from sinners, and made higher than the heavens."[7] Only thus sinless could He have offered Himself to His Father as " a pure host, a holy host, a spotless host."

Inseparable from the priestly character, as we have already mentioned, is the spirit of sacrifice, and it is hardly to be wondered at that this is the spirit which predominates in Jesus the priest. His life on earth from start to finish was a martyrdom of self-abnegation, humiliation, suffering and finally death. From His throne on the cross He came then to His throne on the altar, where He remains amongst us still exercising the priestly functions of sacrifice and mediation. Such a spirit of sacrifice in our Saviour is yet another magnificent manifestation of His boundless love for men ; such love must be found in the heart of every true priest. The heart of the priest must be one from which egoism in all its forms has been excluded ; it must be a heart which beats with a disinterested heroism only for God and for souls. This love Christ our model displayed on the eve of His sacred passion at the moment of performing the supreme act of His priesthood. " Jesus knowing that his hour was come, that he should pass out of this world to the Father : having loved his own who were in the world, he loved them unto the end."[8]

The ideal of our priesthood is Jesus Christ and we shall be true priests only in the measure in which we resemble Him. Simply to be a priest is not enough ; it is of little value to exercise the functions of the priesthood if one does does not live like a priest. The priest is not one who merely holds an office, much less a sinecure, or is clothed in the dignity of a respected calling. The priesthood is a social sacrament, a service, the performance of a work that must be accomplished. One is a priest never for oneself, but only for others.

[7] Heb. vii, 26.
[8] John xiii, 1.

With and like Jesus Christ, therefore, whose work he continues as a collaborator, the priest in every way and at all times will carry out to the full his sacerdotal office, that is to say he will endeavour to glorify God and to save souls. For that, and one cannot meditate on it too often, is the prime reason and the essential purpose of his vocation. The glory of God and the salvation of the world will obsess his spirit and fill his heart to the exclusion of all other feelings. Yet to act like a priest he must have the soul of a priest, as Christ has, that is a soul filled with purity, the spirit of sacrifice and love.

The ambassador of Christ, the minister of His sacraments, in constant contact with the Most Holy Eucharist and the Mystical Body, the priest owes it to himself and to God to preserve an incorruptible purity of soul and body. The victim of his priesthood, he will inherit directly the sorrowful virtues : obedience, humility, poverty, mortification and self-sacrifice. By his vocation he is a being offered and consumed in its performance. " Let him live," says Pius XI, " as a second Christ."

CHAPTER 7

BRETHREN AND MEMBERS OF CHRIST

T HE sovereign and all-embracing perfection of our Saviour is the first foundation of our limitation. We have only to contemplate and copy this Divine ideal to become, in proportion to our resemblance to it, better men, better Christians, better religious, better priests. All holiness is simply a ray of the brilliant light of Christ's perfection.

Another imperative motive for the imitation of our Lord Jesus Christ is to be found in the fact that we have been raised to the supernatural order. As we have been born of God, we are now His adoptive children. By our baptism we have been incorporated in Christ and are living members of His Mystical Body.

We have already touched on this doctrine in connection with Saint Paul's teaching on the Mystical Body, and it seems useful here to go back to that point and examine it more profoundly.

By a miracle of His power and goodness God has raised up mankind to Himself. He has even introduced man to the mystery of His personal life, by bestowing upon him something of His own nature, of His perfection, of His glory and His holiness. It is very clear, though, that to be like God man must act in a God-like way. True resemblance is much more than a superficial likeness—it demands an inward likeness too. The Christian who desires to resemble Christ therefore must practise as perfectly as he can the virtues of Christ.

This special gift which God has given to us of a share in His divine life and in the life of the Blessed Trinity really means that we have been born spiritually of Him. We were not " made " or " created " Christians ; we were conceived and born of God as a child is born of his father and mother. Through this divine generation we resemble not only the Father, but in a very particular way the Son, who like us was conceived and born of the Father.

Our adoptive affiliation with the Father is in fact a wonderful
participation in His natural affiliation with the Divine Word.
What Jesus is by nature we are by grace. Through baptism
we are transformed from the sullied reflection of Adam
into the image of Jesus Christ, the Son of God. Sons of the
same Father, who is God, Christ and the Christian are so to
speak two brothers in their resemblance to the Father and to
each other, their souls welded together in the same family
and fraternal life, each destined to travel the same journey
of light and love to the same paternal home.

We call Christ the " firstborn of every creature,"[1] " the
firstborn from the dead,"[2] " the firstborn amongst many
brethren."[3] Now, as we have become through our spiritual
rebirth in baptism the brothers of our Lord, it is up to us to
prove our kinship by our lives, for as the first-born our Lord
has shown us the way to live. Between Christ and the
Christian there is a union of soul and life which amounts to
what one might call identity. We are born of the Father but
by our baptism we have been grafted on to Christ, incorporated with Him, so that we form only one body, of which
He is the Head and we the members, a full and complete
being, the Mystical Body of Christ.

To be baptised in Christ, as Saint Paul calls it, is not
simply to become subject to Him, like a slave to His master
or a serf to his liege lord, nor to be bound to Him by oath,
like a soldier to his general, nor even consecrated as might
be a temple to a diety. It is far more than all this ; it is
to become *part* of Him, in fact, an *alter Christus*. We are
crucified with Him, buried with Him, we partake of His
death and of His new life in glory, His reign, His inheritance.
It is an ineffable union, likened by Saint Paul to a grafting
which mingles two lives so as to blend and absorb into the
life of the main trunk the life of the grafted branch. It is
a marvellous operation which animates both Christ and
ourselves with the same vital spirit, subject to the same principle of activity. As Saint Paul elsewhere sums it up, we
are clothed in Christ and made to live His life.

---

[1] Coloss. i, 15.
[2] *Ibid.* 18.
[3] Rom. viii, 29.

It is apparent from a study of the dogma of the Mystical Body of Christ that we must so closely imitate our Holy Redeemer that our lives become in effect an unfolding of His life in us. A logical extension of this dogma demands that the members must live in harmony with the Head of the Body—a human head on an animal body would be a monster ; but the law of nature is logical, it works harmoniously. It cannot produce something that is not inherent in itself. No one has ever gathered lilies from a nettle ; only a rose tree bears roses. And thus we may say that the Christian flowers only from Christ, the living tree of eternal life.

CHAPTER 8

THE ILLUMINATIVE WAY

IF the quality and growth of a spiritual life depend in part on the truths which sustain it, none can doubt the sanctifying power of the doctrine of the imitation of Jesus Christ. To put it another way, this is rich and fertile soil in which the soul can take root and derive abundance of strength.

To the pilgrims on the road of salvation and perfection the surest, most direct and happiest route to take is the one recommended by our Lord when He exhorted His hearers, " Follow me " and showed them that He was the " Way." The soul who chooses to follow Christ as his guide and model will find his path endowed with everything to illumine, strengthen and encourage him : for Christ is pure light, indomitable strength, and divine joy and hope.

Perfection rests on Truth. According to evangelical teaching, universal tradition and the life of the Church, the doctrine of imitation is one of the classical and unshakable foundations of sanctity. There is nothing vague about it, no doubtful mysticism, no suggestion of dangerous novelty. Whoever follows in the footsteps of Christ has chosen a road along which he cannot lose his way, for it is flooded with light like the route of a royal procession. One of the chief obstacles to sanctity in the moral order is the lack of light, and the danger of being misguided by false lights such as illusions, ignorance, errors, imprudence or doubts. There are so many spiritual illusions that it is not possible to account for them all. Some are born of the imagination or the passions, of lack of judgment : some are human in origin, others are of the devil. There are illusions about ourselves, our virtues, our faults, our detachments, the illusions of youth, and what are scarcely less harmful, the illusions of maturity and of old age.

Ignorance often accompanies illusions. Do we always fully understand the meaning and purpose of our life's work ?

What is to be made the ideal of the Christian, the religious, the priestly life ? Holiness, fervour, strength, humility, renunciation, poverty, purity, love of the Cross : how do these wonderful words sound to our ears ? Have we measured their greatness or exhausted their full significance ? And how, if not, can we possibly realise an ideal which is not fully understood ? No artist has ever created a masterpiece without first having conceived and seen a vision of it in his mind.

Ignorance, too, is often the near neighbour of error and self-deception. The spirit of the world, so subtle and so contagious, can very easily take on the hue of the supernatural. Very many human maxims are, if not actually heretical, at least unchristian. The clear pure words of the Gospels can be cleverly softened, sweetened, drained of their very pith, completely laicised.

Imprudences are all too common, and all the more serious and incurable since the soul is quite unconscious of them and finds its excuses in perfect good faith ; hasty decisions, heroic resolutions, excess of mortification, outbursts of zeal. Thus what should be a triumphal route is all too often a false track, winding dangerously near to a quagmire, even a precipice.

Who has not experienced doubts of conscience and wondered what to do and wherein lay the will of God ? In certain cases it is extremely difficult to know what to do, or sometimes how to do it. And from a state of anxiety one may fall into a state of scrupulosity as useless as it is distressing.

The sovereign remedy for all these weaknesses and blind spots of the intellect is the imitation of our Lord. Bring the soul face to face with Christ the Sun of Truth, and it is immediately bathed in the splendour of midday, clothed in certitude and transformed into a " child of light." " I am the light of the world," said our Saviour. " He that followeth me, walketh not in darkness, but shall have the light of life."[1] " And you shall know the truth and the truth shall make you free."[2]

[1] John viii, 12.
[2] *Ibid.* 32.

As we contemplate our Lord many of our crude illusions fall away, particularly our illusions of pride, and we see ourselves as we really are, small, insignificant, worthless. Thus we take the first step towards humility, which is the truth about oneself.

Confronted by the holiness of our Saviour, of which we are partaking, and should be trying to reproduce in ourselves, we will then realise that if we wish to preserve the dignity of the Christian, of the religious, of the priest, we shall have to avoid triviality and lukewarmness and turn to a life based on purity, justice and love.

When we meditate upon Jesus, humble, poor, suffering, hard-working, silent and recollected, patient, merciful and dedicated completely to the glory of the Father, we are immediately aware of the beauty of and necessity for virtue. Jesus *is* virtue, living, personified, and in a sense, popularised, that is to say within reach of all souls. Many who would never even know how to define humility or abnegation have perfectly understood the essence of each of these virtues after contemplating Jesus, meek and humble of heart, obedient even unto the death of the Cross.

A piece of speculative teaching will remain always for the majority of people vague and abstruse. There is nothing like a concrete example or a picture to demonstrate a lesson. Christ is the ideal master, because He illustrates His doctrine by His own examples. Before instructing He acted. Of all the books of ascetic theology and mysticism, the most luminous, profound and yet simplest is Christ Himself, if only we would take the trouble to study Him carefully. To Saint Teresa, who was distressed because she had been refused certain spiritual works, our Lord said : " Do not be concerned about it ; I will give you a living book." " I did not fully understand then," the saint goes on, "the meaning of these words, but a few days later they became quite clear to me. The Divine Master was Himself the book wherein I had seen the eternal truths." " He that would fully and with relish understand the words of Christ," says the author of the *Imitation*, " must study to conform his whole life to Him.";[3] True spiritual knowledge, living and fruitful, not mere

---

[3] *Imit.* Book i, ch. 1.

book learning, is to be found in loving contemplation of Christ.

There too will be found the most effective counter-action to the spirit of the times. If we strive to think always like our Master, to adopt His mentality, to become imbued with His teachings, to nourish our souls on His Gospel, we shall acquire an unshakable soundness of judgment by means of which we shall be able, as was our Lord when tempted, to oppose to the maxims of the world and the suggestions of the devil the triumphant words of God.

We should avoid many pitfalls and many errors on our spiritual way if we determined to follow Christ closely, never losing sight of Him on the road, and if before reaching a decision or taking action we realised our need of Him, prayed for His guidance and begged of Him a ray of His divine wisdom. That is the first lesson taught by spiritual directors. As Saint John says, we should not believe every spirit but attach ourselves to the spirit of God.[4] There is no one better than Christ to help us to solve doubts about any course of conduct. It is enough to ask the question : " In my place what would our Lord have said and done ? " for the answer to come firm and reassuring. " For thou lightest my lamp, O Lord : O my God enlighten my darkness."[5]

Mother Eugénie, foundress of the Little Sisters of the Assumption, wrote to Fr. d'Alzon : " We have a little girl of just over four years. If one of us reproaches her about anything, and that she is excusing herself for it, the most powerful reason that we can give her, to point out her mistake, is to ask her if the Infant Jesus would have done that ; she understands wonderfully this idea of the perfect life based on her divine model."

For those souls who are travelling across the plains the way of imitation of Christ is sure and clear. It is not less so for those whom the Holy Ghost has lifted to the heights of contemplation. The important thing is to attach oneself closely to Christ, for the higher the peaks and the steeper the precipices bordering the narrow paths, the greater is the

[4] I. Ep. John, iv, I.
[5] Ps. 17, 29.

necessity for a guide, who can be none other than our Saviour Himself. The imitation of Jesus Christ is at all times and pre-eminently the preparation and introduction, the source, the fruit and the safeguard for perfect contemplation.

The careful reproduction of the ways of Jesus Christ in ourselves is not, of course, conceivable without a complete interior purification ; absence of sin, mastery of the passions, destruction of egoism, in fact the death of the old man. Now, this general purification, a fundamental element of complete sanctity, is one of the essential conditions for the ascendancy of the Holy Ghost. More than that, it may well be a preparation and possibly even a quiet, almost unconscious appeal for the mystical graces. God loves moral purity, and will lean towards the immaculate soul when He is choosing His spouses : not to mention what affection, consolations and gifts He will incline to lavish on those souls who recall to Him His well-beloved Son. His privileged, intimately loved souls are those who are the reproductions of Jesus.

Meditation on the humanity of our Lord leads naturally to contemplation of His divinity.

Actually the normal way to the mystical life can only be by loving imitation of our Saviour. In all its aspects charity tends to union with God, and this union works by a series of progressive changes from imitation to contemplation and thence to fusing of the soul with God. The unique example in the Church of the imitation of Christ burgeoning into a most miraculous mystical life is that of Saint Francis of Assisi. " This adorable Saviour," says Saint Teresa, " who is our all, is the channel through which all good comes to us. Study His life, there is no more perfect model . . . I have studied with care, ever since I understood this truth, the ways of some of the saints, all great contemplatives, and this was their road. Saint Francis proved this to us by his devotion to the Sacred Wounds ; Saint Anthony of Padua by his love for the Child Jesus ; Saint Bernard found his delights in contemplation of the Sacred Humanity of our Saviour ; Saint Catherine of Siena and many others . . . did likewise."

If devotion to the Word Incarnate leads to the highest degrees of contemplation, this in its turn stimulates and reinforces wonderfully the imitation of the Master. From Christ to the Holy Spirit and through the Holy Trinity back to Christ is the flow and surge of this ocean which is called Love. It is the reciprocal engendering of contemplation through imitation, and of further imitation through the fruits of contemplation.

The preoccupation of souls of prayer is to return to Christ and to attach themselves to the practice of His virtues. They know that He is the Good Shepherd and that in following Him the sheep will certainly find the fertile pastures. A spirituality in which Christ is relegated to the shadows, where He is in the background, as it were, is always subject to caution.

Saint Paul instructed the Colossians " unto all the riches of fullness of understanding, unto the knowledge of the mystery. of God the Father and of Christ Jesus in whom are hid all the treasures of wisdom and knowledge."[6] He who possesses Christ has found the sum of all graces ; the grace of light at the beginning and after that the graces of power and perseverance.

---

[6] Coloss. ii, 3.

CHAPTER 9

THE SOURCE OF HEROISM

ON the road of perfection Christ stands out before us not only as a beacon to light the way, but as a force which impels and sustains. He is the Master teaching us, but He is also the Friend, helping and comforting us. In His company and with His example we can develop the soul of the soldier and the heart of the hero ; and it has been truly said : " Sow Christ and you will reap heroism."

Unless it is to become atrophied and finally useless life at all levels has to be maintained by activity, developed by struggle and made fruitful by sacrifice. The spiritual life is no exception ; on the contrary it requires tremendous efforts and indomitable courage. We all know from experience the weakness and cowardice of human nature. Trifles hold us back, and everything frightens us. We may look far and wide for the staunch characters and the finely tempered wills. In the face of sacrifice how many of us simply desert !

The most effective remedy for this moral spinelessness is yet again the imitation of Jesus Christ. At the school of such a Teacher of heroism we may learn to develop our will and to increase our moral force. His example fires and sustains our wills, endowing us with the necessary strength to imitate it, and spreads the desire for sanctity through our hearts. Over and over again in physical battle we have seen that a leader is the making of his troop. If he wants to drive his men out into the mud of the trenches and the danger of death, he simply goes first and they will follow. In the face of his bravery there are few cowards or malingerers.

How many have cried : " Lord, I am tired, worn out, crushed ; I have been calumniated and slandered ; God has abandoned me. Lord, I can do no more ! " And Jesus from the depths of His heart has replied gently : " That is nothing, my child. I too have been weary, crushed, slandered, abandoned before you were, and more than you have ever been. It is nothing, my child. Come and follow

me." And they have followed all the more willingly for
they have loved Him as they have never loved or will love
anyone. Imitation is one of the most authentic acts and
purest forms of love. Nothing is so sweet or so strong as
love, which triumphs over every obstacle. No one leaves
his loved ones, least of all at time of danger. Sacrifice of
oneself is the supreme sign of love. Since then Christ has
given us the first sign, who will dare to refuse Him ? The
heart is the source of this madness which is called heroism,
and in the true and complete imitator of the divine Saviour,
there has to be the stuff of martyrs.

There will always be a champion capable of fighting with
strength and constancy against the forces of egoism. Whoever
wants to be thus the victor over his passions has only to put
on the armour of Jesus Christ. If our passions, says Saint
Augustine, will not yield before the example of Christ then
indeed our case is hopeless. " How could anyone," he asks,
" conquer a pride which was not conquered by the humility
of the Son of God ? " Strength which is needed in reacting
against evil is required too in the action of practising the virtues.
Virtues of their very nature and as the word itself suggests,
are habits of action which are only acquired and developed
in action. Even those which are called " passive " because
they are accompanied by difficult renunciations demand the
maximum of effort and courage. The struggle for virtue
appears all the harder inasmuch as it lasts always, and does
not end until death. For who in the spiritual life has ever
heard of a retreat by the old warriors ! As we see them in
Christ the virtues appear not only luminous but infinitely
attractive and full of beauty. What more natural, then,
than that we should bend all our hearts and energies to
practising them in ourselves.

In the Christian life suffering is both a proof and a mark
of favour for a chosen soul. It is a blessing and a favour
in so far as the soul knows how to suffer without murmur
or revolt, with sweetness and love. The Cross can either
crush or exalt ; transfigure or pervert ; all depends on the
spirit in which it is received. While it is merely an evil
to the soul which blasphemes and rejects, it can shower
infinite blessings on the soul which embraces it and carries

it valiantly. To achieve this the soul simply follows the Saviour. In the face of Christ, bruised, bleeding, scoffed at, who would dare to complain ? It was only in the comtemplation of the Crucified, in the ardent desire to be like Him and to give Him love for love and blood for blood, that all the great lovers of the Cross, the eager martyrs, the self-immolated victims of expiation, the humble penitents, were able to derive the strength to suffer in silence and to die so magnificently. In the steps of the Master who is there who not only could but would desire to climb the road to Calvary, especially as so often we shall find Him again on the road as our Good Samaritan !

During the dark and frosty nights a king of Bohemia used to go out barefoot to visit the sick. Walking behind him one night his exhausted servant began to complain, saying : " I am frozen. I can't go any further."

" Put your feet in the prints of my steps," said the holy man, " and follow me " and lo and behold, by a miracle his footsteps were warm and glowing with light, and the servant's fatigue vanished completely. So too, if we follow Christ, very closely, He will be our light and our strength. To practice the imitation of Christ is to build our lives on His support, to make Him the corner-stone of our spiritual edifice. Jesus is the immovable rock on which to build high and firm, not " on the wisdom of men but on the power of God."[1]

---

[1] I Cor. ii, 5.

CHAPTER 10

BEATITUDE

L IGHT is often the harbinger of joy. In the spring
dawns we hear the twittering of all the birds, and the
sky seems to be the kingdom of happiness, precisely
because it is the abode of continual light : *Lux aeterna.* So
the triumph of strength even though sometimes difficult
in the service of justice is always accompanied by a profound
if austere joy. That is the explanation of why the way of
imitation of Christ is bathed in light and suffused with the
spirit of generosity, and why it is thus revealed as being
actually a source of abundant happiness. Indeed the secret
of happiness lies in the loving imitation of the Incarnate
Word.

In some people's eyes Christianity all too often appears
to retain an exclusive or at least dominant aspect of severity
and grimness. Religion is an intellectual slavery, a moral
servitude which is sustained and buttressed by terror of a
dreadful and eternal place of punishment : the Church is
simply the spiritual form of the totalitarian state.

Nothing could be a greater travesty of Catholicism,
whose true face, radiant and sympathetic, is only seen through
the imitation of Jesus when God the Saviour becomes our
Father, and Christ our Judge becomes our Brother and our
Friend. Then we see that the Church is our mother, and
humanity one mighty and divine family. Christianity demands
discipline, certainly, but infinitely more does it call the heart ;
and though fear should not be entirely eliminated from our
relationship with God, nevertheless it is tempered with hope
and crowned with joy.

The Gospel itself is the Good News, the blessed book.
Vocation to happiness is vocation to Catholicism. The
Church which paradoxically sang in the catacombs over
the graves of the martyrs, has continued to sing over the
graves of her faithful children. The Christian who follows
Christ loyally is like a living harp resounding with joyous

music. There are many sources of profound and inexhaustible joy in the soul which walks the way of the Redeemer and makes Him its companion and guide. There is, for instance, the joy of knowing Him better, of studying Him, of penetrating deeper and deeper every day into the secrets of His interior life, and of unveiling the mysteries of His divinity. When we think how the beauty of a noble landscape, or an encounter with a delightful personality can move us at times to transports of bliss, how much more can we say of the revelation of Christ who is the essence of beauty and the very depths of perfection. Indeed " it is good for us to be here," on our knees in contemplation of Christ ; a rapture which we know is only a prelude to Paradise.

Of all the pleasures those of the heart are the sweetest and most rapturous, and no soul begins to love Christ whose love does not grow until it becomes a veritable fountain of perfect happiness.

> Nor tongue nor pen can show
> The love of Jesus : what it is
> None but His lovers know.

Who clothes himself with Christ has donned the vesture of joy. It is above all the joy of living continually in the closest intimacy of mind and heart with the Beloved, for the constant imitation of Christ presupposes His habitual presence in the soul. The solitary soul is no longer alone. He has a faithful Companion on his road, to talk to, to love, to pray to, and to follow and lean upon. " When Jesus is present all is well, and nothing seems difficult ; . . . if Jesus speak only one word, we feel great consolation . . . Happy hour when Jesus calleth us from tears to joy of spirit . . .to be with Jesus is a sweet paradise . . .Whoever findeth Jesus findeth a good treasure—yea, a good above every good."[1]

But the crowning happiness for the imitator of Christ is in growing to resemble the Son of God, in becoming another Christ. If happiness consists in the fulness of our being and the employment of all our powers, then it is in the imitation of Christ that we shall find our complete fulfilment.

---

[1] *Imit.* Book 2, ch. 8.

By imitating Him we shall possess in Him and through Him all that could possibly complete, satisfy and delight us : wisdom, virtue, love, nobility, holiness, assurance of salvation.

From time to time our Saviour will reveal Himself at the right moment as the unique and incomparable comforter. All of us, in the course of our lives, have had our trials and ordeals : setbacks, sorrows, physical and moral suffering. And our problem when burdened by the cross is how to keep, if not joyful, at least serene. The answer is again, and always, loving imitation of Christ. In company with the Crucified none will complain or despair. For after all He came among us also to heal bruised hearts and dry tears. " Come to me, all you that labour, and are burdened, and I will refresh you."[2] He is happy indeed who lives so constantly in the presence of Christ that in hours of anguish he is able, like the disciple John, to rest his head above the very Heart of Jesus, and savour in silence the sweetness of the evangelical beatitudes : " Blessed are they that mourn. . . . Blessed are they that suffer persecution . . . Blessed are the poor in spirit . . . Blessed are the meek . . ." To suffer with Jesus Christ, like Jesus Christ and for Jesus Christ is in itself a joy, austere indeed, but nevertheless the joy which the first Christians, the Apostles, knew and loved. " And they indeed went from the presence of the council, rejoicing that they were accounted worthy to suffer reproach for the name of Jesus."[3] The saying which Christ addressed to His disciples He repeats still to His imitators : " Your heart shall rejoice ; and your joy no man shall take from you."[4] We, the new pilgrims to Emmaus, anxious, weary, discouraged, may if we so choose meet on our journey and keep with us until death the faithful Companion who will be our light, our strength and the joy of our hearts.

The source of light and strength and joy : that is the way of imitation, which is thus the royal road to sanctity. Limited and sinful creatures as we are, we could not possibly grow to the stature of our Redeemer except by placing ourselves in His presence, bending all our moral energies towards

---

[2] Matt. xi, 28.
[3] Acts v, 41.
[4] John xvi, 22.

achieving the measure of His perfection and lifting ourselves
to the height of His virtues. Among all the forms of the
spiritual life, and they are very numerous, the way of imitation
of Christ stands out, and one cannot repeat it too often, as
the surest, the easiest and the most direct. It is the evangelical
way, outlined and indicated by the Saviour Himself. It is the
eminently Christian way, in which we can adore God in spirit
and in truth, and in which religion is revealed to us by His
own profound spirit and divine heart. It is the traditional
way, frequented throughout the centuries by all the generations, along which the flowers of sanctity bloom ceaselessly
in all their variety and fragrance. It is the catholic way,
that is to say it is universal ; the common way, on to which
every man no matter what his age or state, social position
or natural inclinations can venture always without danger
and inevitably with profit.

One day, during the mass *Salve sancta Parens* Saint Mech-
tilde asked the Blessed Virgin Mary to bestow on her true
sanctity. Our Lady responded : " If you wish for true
sanctity, get close to my Son ; He is holiness itself, sanctifying
everything . . . Unite yourself with His virtues which will
ennoble and elevate your own . . . so that your soul will be
nourished with the best spiritual sustenance, the Word of
God, and so that it will be steeped in the delights which it
will find in Him, namely the example which He will give it
to imitate . . . That way you will truly become a saint."

The happy souls are those to whom the Spirit of God
has given the power to understand and savour and put into
practice this wonderful teaching. They have found in it
the secret of perfection and have themselves become so
eminently holy that they can offer to the world the appearance of being " other Christs." " He that abideth in me,
and I in him, the same beareth much fruit : for without me
you can do nothing."[5] The imitating soul has made of
Christ the faithful Companion of her entire existence.
Through contemplation, prayer and love, in action or in
quietude, she lives with Him, like Him and in Him, thereby
reaping a harvest of virtues and a wealth of merit.

---

[5] John xv, 5.

CHAPTER II

HOW TO FOLLOW CHRIST

ALL spiritual " ways," great or small, are influenced by contemporary spiritual thought. People are inclined to ask whose line of thought this is, or who recommended that.

However, in all branches of human activity some method or system prevails so there is no reason to object to it in the moral and supernatural order. We have systems of learning, systems of teaching, systems of design and painting, systems even of sport . . . why then should it be out of place to have a system of sanctification? The scholar, the artist, the craftsman, each leans towards his own style and *modus vivendi* be it good, bad or indifferent. He has, or he can have, his own particular method of working. This method, which may be defined as the science and the art of work, is a collection of logical rules and technical processes designed to simplify and co-ordinate the work and make it at the same time less laborious and more productive. Everyone knows from experience that careful organisation and correct management will double production. This obtains also in the intellectual order, both artistic and moral, although it is not so long since people smiled indulgently at a certain little Way of Spiritual Childhood, for which today they have the most profound admiration. Such a reaction may be blamed on ignorance, or prejudice, or a combination of both.

The application of " method " to the work of sanctification is supported by the great theological principle that grace does not destroy nature but perfects it. It exploits our human powers and natural virtues and turns them to good account towards holiness. There is every reason, then, why the work of our religious and sacerdotal transformation should be carried out in a thoughtful and methodical spirit.

So many of us seem to be attacked by a sort of moral

inertia or somnolence, and fail to achieve sanctity. There are the complicated souls, who are too tied up in knots to grow and develop ; the immature ones who never leave the spiritual cradle ; or those which like a stunted shrub bear only occasional and shrivelled fruits for their flowers have never developed from the bud. How do we explain these sad, and sometimes scandalous aberrations among those who are apparently living the spiritual life ? How account for their abortive and degenerate development ? There are many causes, in fact, and among the most serious are to be included an absence of clear direction and a lack of common sense. To hold to some kind of system means that we have a guide when, alone, without maps or charts, we enter upon the narrow way of the spiritual life. It is a way full of pitfalls, surrounded by precipices and criss-crossed by unknown paths and routes, immersed often in thick mist or heavy darkness. We hesitate, groping, go forward a little, turn back, mark time—and sometimes get lost altogether.

Moral mediocrity and banality of soul are often born of ignorance or error. This is not due to lack of grace ; we have that at hand any time we want it, rich and powerful. Nor is it due, except in very rare cases, to any lack of good-will, even though this may often leave much to be desired in matters of force or generosity. No, what is lacking almost inevitably in most of our spiritual " invalids " is " the science and the art of sanctity." They have either never properly understood the work of self-sanctification, or else they have understood but have set about it in the wrong way. Instead of embarking on this wonderful enterprise in an ordered and consequently fruitful manner, the best they can achieve is an improvised, clumsy and unfortunately sterile effort ; so they achieve only the rough draft of the apprentice in place of the finished work of the master.

However, if methods of holiness, like methods of prayer, have their convinced supporters, they have also, especially in times of pseudo-mysticism, their stubborn opponents. " Methods of sanctity," these will say, " deprive the soul if not of its liberty at least of its spontaneity. The essential work of grace, which is the sanctification of our souls, cannot any more than could grace itself, be subjected in its origin and development to our petty recipes, and hampered by our stereotyped blueprints. The Master of the spiritual life is the Holy Ghost who inspires where and when and how He wills. We do not have to show Him the way and He does not require our signposts. Nothing is so great, so flexible, so joyful, so overpowering as the Gospel ; to what benefit, then, are the attempts to reduce it to dry and didactic formulae, or to cast it into a common mould out of which the saints ought to issue in a row ? Let us live the Gospel, simply, lovingly, joyously, in the holy liberty of the children of God. That is quite enough."

This is a specious objection. That certain narrow methods, over-complicated or even excellent in themselves but badly understood and wrongly followed, become to the soul nothing more than a restraining force holding back its flight, no one will attempt to deny. But apart from these, there are many others, simple and amply flexible, which wisely employed will not discourage the spontaneity of souls nor hamper them in their aspirations to the higher planes of the spiritual life. Who has ever pretended to make rules and regulations for grace, or attempted to bridle the Holy Ghost ? Yet it is necessary—and this is as much a matter of prudence as of efficacy—that we ensure our powerful co-operation with grace and our perfect docility towards the Holy Ghost : and that can best be achieved by possessing a spirit enlightened by methodical or disciplined effort and a will which has been methodically strengthened and tempered.

But, someone will surely reply, the Christian and religious world is full of the splendid souls of many saints who never knew, suspected the existence of or practised any method of sanctification. Is this, however, quite as true as those who advance it would like to believe ? That there have been many souls who have reached the heights of sanctity without ever having studied this or that classic method, or consciously followed this or that spiritual way, no one is going to doubt. But that these very souls, through certain chosen habits, by the special practice of this or that virtue, by the particular form which they succeeded in giving to their interior life and to their exterior practice, were actually forming an empirical method of perfection, completely personal and sometimes very original, no one can doubt either ; even though they did not set out explicitly to do so, nor did they ever express their method in precise formulae. Even if it were possible to enter upon the spiritual life without a system or to make a certain progress in it, still it would be necessary to prove that we should not make a better start or steadier progress by making use of some method. Still less has anyone the right to set up against the judicious use of such methods the doctrinal authority and personal experience of the Doctors and Saints of the Church, since some of them have been the very innovators, teachers and illustrious practitioners of them.

Among the innumerable methods of self-sanctification that there are, the imitation of Christ occupies a place apart. It is as old as Christianity itself, as we have seen, yet it has been able throughout the centuries to adapt itself to the times, to present a fresh and new appearance and to expand and develop under new forms. The method of imitation of Christ which we propose has a fourfold character : it is explicit, universal, particular and austere.

Right at the beginning it is apparent that there is a distinction between formal or explicit imitation and material or implicit imitation. How are we to know which is which ?

We recall first of all that Christ, the God-Man, is the archetype and at the same time the origin of all created perfection, the necessary and universal example of all activity in the order of nature as well as in the order of grace. What is the supernatural life, if not the full and radiant reproduction of the life of Jesus Christ Himself " Of His fulness we have all received . . . " " I live, now not I, but Christ liveth in me."

Whether we think it or not, whether we wish it or not, by our very existence and in our bearing we betray in some measure a resemblance to Jesus Christ. But the resemblance is by no means a facsimile in our case, any more than it would be in the case of children who resemble their father both physically and temperamentally even though they do not in any way imitate him. Imitation implies a great deal

more than resemblance ; it demands a conscious and deliberate
copying of a model. To reproduce Christ in ourselves,
unconsciously and involuntarily, would be implicit imitation,
material and indirect. To reproduce Him through profound and sincere contemplation, in other words to " rein-
carnate " Him in our souls and in our lives, that is explicit
imitation, formal and direct : and it is of our own doing.
When the painter is confronted by a great masterpiece he
studies it carefully and tries to put it all down again on his
canvas, to make a perfect copy of it. The imitation of Christ
is exactly the same work, translated to the supernatural
sphere. In the words of Saint Gregory Nazianzen everyone is the painter of his own life : the model is Christ ;
the tool is our own will, and the colours are the virtues.

Next we shall study the characteristic of *universality* in
the work of imitation of Christ.

Our method is addressed to every soul without exception,
the Christian layman, the religious, the priest. No matter
what the age, situation, vocation of anyone may be : what
his degree of intellectual or moral development : any and
all, young girls, mothers of families, men of the world,
priests, can within the framework which we shall demonstrate,
set out to imitate Christ. While there may be certain aristocratic methods of spirituality which appeal to an élite, our
method of the imitation of Christ, though far from being
vulgar or trivial, has this in common with the use of prayer
and the sacraments, that it is essentially popular, of the people,
in that it is open to all men of good will. Every soul, whether
great or small, can make use of this method without difficulty,
but certainly not without profit.

The object of our imitation is Christ, whole and complete,
in His Humanity and His Divinity : His life, His virtues,
His perfections, His example, His mysteries, His inner dispositions. The practice of some dozen virtues, one for
each month of the year, of which we shall say more pre-
sently, does not exhaust the content of our approach. It
constitutes a portion of the programme, and we shall simply
indicate, without necessarily imposing it, how this may help
our work by defining our Model all the more clearly. It
would not help at all, however, if any one aspect of our

method were to exclude the rest to the point of eclipsing its universality.

To confine oneself to the exclusive practice of one special virtue would be to misunderstand our line of thought and so to falsify our method. The practice of a particular virtue every month with the maximum of goodwill and generosity must not at the same time deceive us into a false sense of having reduced the whole work of imitation to a simple formula : this would only dangerously lessen and sterilise the whole method.

We are going to model ourselves upon our Lord, then, by imitating His Life, example and virtues, His mysteries and inner dispositions, as we have already said. There are different aspects to His life. There is His life as the Word in the bosom of the Father ; His life as the carpenter of Nazareth, humble, poor, solitary and needy ; there is the public life, travelling from place to place, hard-working and austere, which culminated in the bloody sacrifice of Golgotha. Then there are the many ways in which He gave us examples to follow : examples of His silence, sweetness and patience, His mercy and His zeal. There are all His immense virtues, human and divine, such as His innocence, His ardent hatred of evil, His self-control, His filial piety, His obedience, chastity, prudence, force, justice, temperance, tenderness towards His Mother, passion for the glory of His Father.

Study of His interior life, its abnegation, adoration, religion, self-abandonment, shows us a radiance of which His outward life was the merest efflorescence. Finally there are the mysteries of His Incarnation, Birth, Presentation at the temple, Transfiguration, Passion, Death, Resurrection and Ascension. All these mysteries of the life of Jesus Christ can be our mysteries too, to the precise extent to which we are prepared to be born again, to grow and develop, to die and come to life by Him and with Him and in Him. The mystery of the Christian life is one and the same mystery as the life of Jesus Christ,

For our lives to become a permanent exercise in " christification " we must follow Him in everything, through everything, and at all times. There must not be a page of our lives which does not bear His stamp : our outward works,

our inward acts, every sign of activity about us will reflect
Him. We will use everything, thoughts, sentiments,
words, sufferings, prayers, study, preaching, teaching, whatever are the duties of our state even down to the most banal
acts such as eating, drinking, relaxing and sleeping, as blows
of the chisel which will all the time be carving the image
of our Redeemer out of the block of our being. Throughout
the day we shall carry on the work of imitation, not in fits
and starts, but steadily without break or rest, so that if anyone
were to ask us point blank what we were doing, we should be
able to reply without hesitation and with perfect truth : " I
am imitating Christ." Little by little this will result in a very
wonderful and divine transformation of our inner powers
into those of our Lord Himself : our intelligence, will,
heart and conscience will reflect Him as would a mirror the
sun, so that our entire being will undergo a mystical transfiguration in the holiness of Jesus.

Our Lord is like some prodigious symphony and rare
indeed is the artist who can sight-read and interpret such
a great work at first view. Obviously then a very special
preparation and study is called for : a study as it were of the
score, part by separate part, and our method of imitation
involves just such a process. We imitate the whole Christ,
it is true, but to facilitate this tremendous undertaking, we have
divided it and spaced it out so that we set before ourselves,
as the object of our resolutions and best efforts, twelve of His
virtues, to be attempted in turn throughout the twelve months.

It may be objected here that we should be content to imitate
Christ's virtues in general, according to how circumstances
require the practice of them, and that we could bend our
daily lives to the imitation of Christ within that scope.
The answer to that is that such purely general and occasional
acts of imitation run the danger of becoming lost altogether,
in the general turmoil of life, and thereby certain important
aspects of the spiritual life tend to end up as routine matters
or to be lost in the shadows to the detriment of the soul.
Those who pretend to stick to the broad lines of the moral
physiognomy of our Lord, without paying too much
attention to detail, run the risk of reproducing instead of a
true portrait, merely a rough sketch of their model.

On the other hand, to ask at every moment or at the start of each new task what, in these particular circumstances Christ would have thought, said or done, is to put upon oneself a very heavy burden of complication, with the probable consequence of impotence or complete ineffectiveness. Whereas to set about the work of imitation systematically by cataloguing all the virtues and selecting for each month of the year one in particular to practise, carefully secures, in our opinion, the maximum return, variety and interest for the soul who tries it.

What are these twelve virtues of which we speak ? Here they are, according to Saint Alphonsus Liguori : " Faith, hope, charity towards God, love of our neighbour, poverty, purity of body and mind, obedience, sweetness and humility, mortification, recollection, prayer, abnegation and love of the Cross." This short enumeration does not of course exhaust the complete list of virtues of our Blessed Lord. Their genealogical tree has a thousand branches and each is thick with leaves. Nor need we repeat that this whole programme thus analysed and detailed is in no sense obligatory. Here above all full liberty must be allowed to each individual soul, though we ought at the same time to ensure that the use of such liberty be guided by prudence. Each of us must make his own choice, but it should be a judicious one, for though all these virtues are good, they may not all be excellently suited to our own abilities and scope.

We must note at the outset, however, that certain virtues such as faith, hope, charity, humility, mortification, piety and recollection, for the very reason that they are a fundamental and essential basis for the spiritual life, are demanded at all times of everyone. To exclude any of them would be not only a grave omission but a serious mistake, for in the absence of these corner-stones the solidity of the spiritual edifice would be materially threatened. But having made that original selection, we should then base our choice of the virtues to imitate on the exigencies of our state of life or vocation. The perfection of the lay Christian is not that of the priest, nor the sanctity of the contemplative identical with that of the missionary.

Following the example of our Lord, we shall all practise

virtue, but not the same virtues, or at least not in the same way or to the same degree. We shall become imitators of Christ the Ideal, even at the risk of becoming specialists in our attachment to this or that aspect of the life or that trait of the soul of our divine Saviour. Orders and Congregations, for example, for the most part have their own special spirit and characteristic virtues. So it must be in conformity with that spirit, within the framework of that Rule and the duties of that state that each of us will set about the choice and realisation of the virtues we intend to imitate. The Jesuit will imitate Christ as a Jesuit, the Capuchin as a Capuchin, the Carmelite as a Carmelite and so on ; thus achieving a vital and interesting variety of reproductions of the one unique Model. Wisdom too should guide our choice, by taking count of the variable and successive states of our souls, the demands on grace, exceptional difficulties, such as occasions of sin, internal crises or grave temptation, which we shall certainly encounter on the road. At some stage of our spiritual life, as chance circumstances may dictate, extra pressure in the practice of any particular virtue may be demanded. If the necessity or the danger arise, we should know how to modify the plan of our campaign. The main thing is to be able always to go to the assistance of the hardest pressed, to leave everything in order to support the barrier which may crumble, the house which may burn down.

Each month, then, to have a special virtue " on the stocks " for imitation is the third characteristic of our method.

CHAPTER 12

ON THE ROAD TO CALVARY

TO the other characteristics of our method of sanctification we add one which we believe important enough
to occupy an entire chapter, namely austerity. The
Christ we propose to imitate is the Christ preached by
Saint Paul, Christ Crucified. It will not be surprising,
therefore, that the shadow of Calvary will lie across the
lives of all who follow Christ our way, and that the holy
Cross of Jesus will be seen at every crossroad on the journey.
Imitation of our Lord's virtues, example, interior states and
mysteries is sufficient for us to attain sanctity provided we
realise that all these words are written, as it were, in blood.
It is a life of continual martyrdom.

Imitation of Himself, to which our Lord invites us, and
which the Apostles taught, is based entirely upon renunciation. All the great and time-honoured devotions to the
Sacred Passion, the Holy Eucharist, the Sacred Heart, imply
in their object, their practice and their fruit the ideal and
the love of sacrifice.

Later we shall see the triumphant Christ face to face, and
if we have been truly faithful we shall resemble Him, but
for the present while we remain earth-bound, the Christ
we know is the Man of Sorrows. He is the Crucified,
hanging upon the Cross, found everywhere in the Christian
world, in the church and the home, at wayside shrines,
pressed to the lips of the dying and held in the hands of
sinners. Christ for us poor human beings struggling and
suffering here below, is the Host, our daily Bread, the Victim
offered on our altars ; He is our Brother and our Friend,
revealing His Heart to us, but it is a bleeding heart, surrounded
with thorns and surmounted by a cross. That is the Christ,
infinitely sorrowful, who invites us to contemplate, to love
and to imitate Him. Obviously it would be impossible
to conceive the Christian, the religious and the sacerdotal
life other than in terms of sacrifice, which is in fact the very
source and essential of its success.

Spiritual life is born of the death of self. Before we can rise again to a divine life in Christ we must first die as He did. The new man can rise only on the ruins of the old. Or to put it another way, virtue can only grow and flourish in the ground which has been opened by the plough, broken by the harrow and watered by the sweat of the labourer. To struggle, to suffer but finally to triumph is the Christian destiny. "If any man would come after me, let him deny himself, and take up his cross and follow me."[1] Every soul is born to the divine life under the shadow of the Cross, or rather on the Cross itself. Baptism is a birth, but it is also a type of death and burial, for in order to be born into the Christian life it is necessary to die and be buried with Jesus. Our spiritual life, therefore, is actually a resurrection and obviously before one can rise again one has to die first. Even more obvious is it that sacrifice is the very soul of the religious state. If the Christian is already an offshoot of the Cross, how much more so is the religious, called by vocation to the very perfection of Christianity.

He must be poor to the extent of detachment from all created things ; chaste to the extent of complete virginity ; obedient to the extent that he is a willing slave even unto death. It is not possible to fulfil these conditions without martyrdom. Whoever embraces the religious state thereby extends himself on the full length of the Cross, and his three vows nail him there. In other words, religious communities are to be embodiments of the Cross.

However, it is above all the priest who will bear most deeply the marks of the sacrificial victim. Participating, as he does, in all the dignity and power of the great high Priest, invested with the same functional powers, Christ's co-operator in the work of the Redemption, the priest is in truth another Christ. *Sacerdos alter Christus*, and his priesthood is in fact the prolonging and extension of the very priesthood of Jesus. But Christ willed to be the Victim of His own priesthood and the Host of His own sacrifice. *Sacerdos et Hostia.* There is the identification between the priest, the sacrifice and the victim, and so the conclusion at once wonderful and terrible is borne inescapably upon us,

---

[1] Matt. xvi, 24.

with all the force of centuries' tradition, that the priest, every priest, by virtue of his unique and magnificent calling, must offer himself as victim like and with the Priest Jesus Christ.

Priests, reproduce in yourselves, therefore, what you do daily at the altar !² Sons of Calvary, it is to you especially that Jesus spoke the words : " And he that taketh not up his cross nor followeth me, is not worthy of me."³ But he is indeed the worthy priest who can say with Saint Paul : " I now rejoice in my sufferings . . . and fill up those things that are wanting of the sufferings of Christ in my flesh, for his body which is the church."⁴ If we endeavour to envisage the full development of the Christian and especially of the priestly life, we shall notice that the role of sacrifice becomes intensified and that the need for the hard and difficult imitation of Christ crucified is impressed with all the greater force. That perfection which consists, again in the words of Saint Paul, in " attaining the unity of Faith, and of the knowledge of the Son of God, unto a perfect man, unto the measure of the age of the fulness of Christ."⁵ is like a flower which blooms only in the ardent warmth of suffering. Sanctity, love, sacrifice : these are the three divine energies which always bear the soul up with the same *élan* and beat with the same rhythm. " Greater love than this no man hath, that a man lay down his life for his friends "⁶ : and if not called upon for his life, then at least some drops of his blood. Everyone who knows the meaning of love in any sense knows well also the meaning of suffering. Like certain aromatic plants, the more the heart is crushed the greater the perfume of love ascending from it. All the great hearts, beginning with the Hearts of Jesus and Mary, have been the hearts of sufferers. The saints have all cherished a desire, even a passion for sacrifice, for the " folly " of their love has led them inevitably to the " folly of the cross."

There is one more reason which explains and justifies the

---

² Menti Nostrae.
³ Matt. x, 38.
⁴ Coloss. i, 24.
⁵ Eph. iv, 13.
⁶ John xv, 13.

austere aspect of our method of imitation of Christ, and that is the extension, or better still, the sudden quickening into creative life in the Church of the idea of reparation. Under the benign guidance of the Holy Spirit there has been an upsurge in recent times of congregations and of individual souls bent on the work of reparation. The devotion to the Sacred Heart, for instance, is essentially inspired by the idea of reparation. Ever since the first rumblings of materialism, of agnosticism, of laicism and atheism, of all the revolutionary and diabolical forces which threaten to submerge our society, a multitude of generous souls have offered themselves as victims and hosts in a great movement of reparation ; for since the sacrifice of Calvary, we repeat, the great work of reparation continues to be sacrifice.

And so, all souls who have dedicated themselves either by the duty of their state or by a special call of grace to this apostolate, will realise that in the imitation of Christ crucified they will find not only light and comfort, but the greatest and most powerful way to fulfil their destiny.

There is a certain tendency against which we should be on our guard, to react against this austerity. It has a slight tinge of " naturalism," which while not condeming, for such would be heresy, the role of penance and mortification, of humility, obedience and renunciation, tends at the same time to minimise their effectiveness, and in fact to recommend almost exclusively the active virtues of strength, courage, devotion, zeal, and the spirit of enterprise and of conquest. At the other extreme we must also guard against spiritual illusions and mystical adventures. Without sufficient ascetic preparation it is easy to believe oneself called to superior heights of prayer, and to start rushing headlong, while still a beginner, into the routes followed by the saints, without the purification of suffering obtained through arduous contemplative thought and prayer, as is enjoined by all the masters. However, the remedy for the excessive enthusiasm of human zeal or the romantic piety of the beginner on the road to sanctity, and all the errors engendered by a false mysticism, is still and all the time the faithful imitation of Jesus Christ, the Crucified.

CHAPTER 13

KNOWLEDGE OF JESUS CHRIST.

ANY effective method of setting out to achieve an object is, as we have already seen, a combination of science and art, that is a collection of logical rules and technical processes. The method of self-sanctification by imitation of Christ is no exception to this rule and is, in fact, greatly advanced by the sensible application of certain laws and processes which are really the fundamental principles of the spiritual life. For example, let us examine first of all what we shall call the 'Law of Contemplation' from the point of view of its scope and value. We shall define it as follows :

The perfect imitation of Jesus Christ presupposes a thorough, profound and loving knowledge of Him.

We postulate this 'Law of Contemplation' by reason of its very nature as the basis for our method. Outside of such knowledge no one could conceive the explicit, total, particular and austere imitation that we have previously defined as remotely possible. One could no more follow closely in the footsteps of the Saviour without it than a blind man could reproduce a painting of a landscape. Nor will a mere apprehension suffice ; it must be deep and positive knowledge, almost in fact a vision. Perfect imitation demands perfect knowledge.

What is required right from the outset is to know the full Christ, God and Man, human and divine. It is necessary to study His multiple and wonderful relationship with the Father and the Holy Ghost, with the Church and with souls. Christ is everywhere : in the bosom of the Father, in the tabernacle, in the Christian soul, even in the very flowers of the field. He is everywhere . . . sustaining all, quickening all, epitomising all, Divinity and Humanity, the created and the uncreated. " Christ is all, and in all," says Saint Paul.[1]

---

[1] Coloss. III, 2

Such thorough, complete knowledge is necessary to complete and thorough imitation. The fulness of our likeness to Christ depends entirely on our "christological" knowledge : the greater its light the greater the virtue engendered in us. Christ is like some wondrous haunt of ineffable beauty into which we must enter with loving appreciation, so that we may scrutinise and then reproduce in infinite detail all the marvels we shall find. A rapid or distracted glance can reflect only the most superficial and haphazard likeness of our Saviour. To His imitators Christ should appeal like someone facing them in an ever-growing light which gradually throws up into striking relief every detail of His moral aspect. Yet how many of us know Him so little ; to how many of us He is no more than the vague blur that He was to the disciples who glimpsed Him in the morning mist, and we simply say with them : " It is an apparition."[2] One of the first graces we need to ask for, is that recommended by Saint Ignatius Loyola of "knowing Christ intimately in order to love Him the more ardently and follow Him the more faithfully." Otherwise we shall only, as we said before, reproduce a mere sketch of Jesus our Model instead of a true portrait.

However, the most intimate revelation of the nature of Jesus Christ will not inspire us to a true imitation unless we are moved by love. Imitation of Christ is like a flower which can bloom only in the light ; the warm sunlight of love, not the brilliant but frigid starlight of the intellect. There have been many learned theologians indeed who would make but poor reflections of Christ. Purely speculative study is a sterile thing, whereas a loving research into truth is fruitful. Let us study Jesus our Model " in all wisdom and understanding," so that we may arrive at a knowledge of Him which is full indeed, but which overflows with love, since it is not at all enough to apprehend Him intellectually. We must give Him welcome in our hearts, for our theology should be a science *mentis et cordis*, intellectual and affective.

In the spiritual life the love of the soul for Jesus Christ is a *sine qua non* of the success of its imitation. A child imitates his father and mother because he loves them ; a pupil similarly

---

[2] Matt. xiv, 26.

imitates the teacher whom he loves and admires. On the other hand a stranger will leave all of us completely indifferent; it would never occur to us to model our lives on him, simply because we do not know him. To achieve such knowledge and love of our Saviour implies a constant pre-occupation with Him, from which will develop a profound desire for complete union with Him. Then, just as the bud will blossom when the stem is filled with the rising sap, the heart full of love for Christ will flower, and the flower will be Christ.

When we love our friends we find ourselves delighting in their intellectual and moral abilities, and sometimes even, for love is blind, in their faults. We take a pride in assessing their talents, their learning, their virtues. These two emotions of admiration and pride frequently awaken in us, often without our conscious awareness, a strong desire to reproduce in ourselves what pleases us so much in our kindred spirits. It is an instinctive need to bring ourselves into still closer communion with them, to be all the more worthy of the return of our affection. Equally, such love will hardly survive the revelation of corruption or faithlessness. A friendship thus dishonoured is nearly always a friendship lost. It follows that if we wish to love Christ and enjoy His friendship it will be necessary for us to make ourselves worthy of Him, and by the imitation of His virtues to make our lives as like Him as we can. A friendship commences and is sustained only when the two people concerned find that they have something in common and can approach life from the same viewpoint. That was why Christ in His great love for us decided *to resemble us*, " being made in the likeness of men,"[3] and it is also why, through our love for Christ we must set ourselves to resemble Him, and by imitating Him become other Christs.

Between our love for Christ and our work of imitating Him there is complete interdependence. The deeper our love, the more faithful our imitation. Imitation is the ultimate fulfilment of love, it is love in its most beautiful form, its most vigorous expression and its most divine and delightful fruit. Finally we must not forget that without

[3] Phil. ii, 17.

a generous love for our Saviour it would be extremely difficult
to give to our imitation of Him the ultimate and supreme
distinctive characteristic, the spirit of sacrifice. The reproduction in our souls of Jesus our Model, unless it were thus
sustained by a deep love would become a desperate effort,
doomed to failure. Love alone can produce heroism, and
the Cross will not remain standing unless it is firmly planted
in the heart.

Having reached a certain degree of intimacy and love,
we shall proceed very naturally to a direct and constant
contemplation of Jesus Christ. As a copyist must return
a hundred or indeed a thousand times to the masterpiece he
is working from, for a quick glance precedes every touch
he makes, so we too must never lose sight for a moment
of Jesus our Model. Our imitation necessitates a continual
tête à tête with our Saviour, a rapid and frequent recollection
of His character and of His virtues, and our thoughts should
fly constantly back to Him like the bee to the flower. To
forget for a moment is to cease to imitate Him.

If we would live like Christ we must live with Christ,
maintaining unbroken our contact with His spirit and His
will ; we must, in other words, lead a life of constant recollection of which the main purpose is habitual thought on
Jesus Christ. For the soul who would imitate Christ the
principal study is the study of Christ. Happy is the soul
which can say with Saint Paul : " For I judged not myself
to know anything among you but Jesus Christ, and him
crucified."[4]

In answer to the question : " What is your favourite
book ? " Sister Elizabeth of the Carmel at Dijon replied :

" The soul of Christ. In it I learn all the secrets of the
Father who is in heaven."[5]

---

[4] I Cor. ii, 2.
[5] Philipon : *The Spiritual Doctrine of Sister Elizabeth of the Trinity* (Mercier).

CHAPTER 14

PRAYER

PRAYER is one of the principal bulwarks for those who set out to sanctify themselves by imitating Christ. He becomes for us the centre of attraction, the focal point of light and love. *Da ergo Christo locum*, says à Kempis, and we must give Him His place in our hearts and in our wills, in all our activities but especially and above all in our souls that the thought of Him may possess them and direct all we do. We must try to turn all prayer, the Way of the Cross, the Rosary, the Mass, the Breviary, visits to the Blessed Sacrament, meditations, reading and study to the purpose of perfecting our knowledge, increasing our intimacy and drawing nearer to the actual presence of Jesus Christ. Prayer thus directed is richly rewarding for the imitator of our Lord, because it is full of Him, and it becomes the least difficult and most fruitful of all forms of prayer for religious and priest, and for all interior souls.

There are the endless beauties and wonders of His birth, life, passion and death, His virtues and His mysteries to fill our thoughts. "Above all," says Saint Francis de Sales, "I recommend to you mental prayer, the prayer of the heart, and particularly that which concerns the life and Passion of our Lord. By making Him often the subject of your meditation, your whole soul will be filled with Him. You will learn His ways and frame all your actions according to His model."[1] To help us we have the Gospels. Of all the books and manuals of meditation the Gospels are obviously unique, for every page of them is filled with revelations of the Incarnate Word. They are the substantial food to which we return continually, and which eventually satisfies us to the exclusion of all others.

Even in meditations on other subjects, such as the four last things, the spiritual life, the religious or the sacerdotal state, there is no reason why we should not there also seek and find

---

[1] Introduction to the Devout Life : Part II, ch. 1.

Jesus Christ.   He is the Truth upon which all truths con-
verge as their centre and their origin, and while we meditate
upon one truth we can follow it back as one would trace a river
to its source, so that it will end in contemplating Truth itself.
Instead of delaying over abstract considerations, if we were
to go direct to the Truth we seek, embodied and personified
in the soul and the life of Christ, such Truth would most
certainly acquire sharper relief, greater beauty and profounder
attraction for us.

"The principal object of prayer," says Cardinal Mercier
to his seminarians, "will not then be to ripen abstract truth
for the sake of its moral value, its principal object will be
our living God, Jesus Christ our Lord, His inner dispositions
and His works."

For example : Meditation on Death.

If we wish to meditate upon death we know the full range
of the many aspects of this theme.   But suppose that we
were to take as the subject of our meditation : *Death and
Jesus Christ.*   We now have the inexhaustible study of His
thoughts, His teachings, His attitude towards death.   We
shall find them in the Gospel : "Wherefore be you also ready
because at what hour you know not the Son of Man will
come "[2] "Watch ye, therefore, because you know not the
day nor the hour."[3]   His thoughts, His wishes and His
fears : "With desire I have desired to eat this pasch with
you,"[4] and "My Father, if it be possible, let this chalice
pass from me."[5]   We find there, too, the account of His
attitude to His own death, the heroism of His acceptance of
it, a heroism transformed by love into sacrifice for the glory
of the Father and the redemption of mankind.   We will
endeavour to adopt the same thoughts and attitude towards
the death which awaits us when the work of our imitation of
Christ has been completed.

Another example : Marian Devotion.

We may wish to meditate on another theme, that of
devotion to Mary.   Theologically and ascetically at this

---

[2] Matt. xxiv, 44.
[3] *Id.* xxv, 13.
[4] Luke xxii, 15.
[5] Matt. xxvi, 39.

point we could dissertate on the cult of the Blessed Virgin, establishing its origins and analysing its many elements, but we prefer to wonder at and love its glorious flowering in the soul of Jesus Christ, the first of Mary's devotees. Let us consider, then, instead, how He venerated His Mother and exalted her from the instant of her immaculate conception to the triumph of her coronation in heaven ; how He surrounded her by His unique and ineffable love, and associated her with Him in the mighty work of the Redemption. Let us think on how He confided Himself absolutely to her tender devotion, from the moment that He descended into her virginal womb until He lay dead in her arms at the foot of the Cross. So, once again we shall find that our filial devotion to Mary has its model in the veneration, the love and the trust of Jesus in His mother.

Thus based on contemplation of Jesus Christ, prayer takes on the appearance of a very natural and intimate conference with the Master Himself. If we meet Christ we must surely feel the need to talk with Him, and so meditation upon Christ quickly becomes meditation with Christ. Yet too often our prayers become overladen with distractions and weariness, because they are too one-sided. We cultivate the soliloquy, as it were, and forget the dialogue, and the soliloquy is a difficult and tedious form. To pray well we must talk with our Lord and then listen and perhaps we should listen more frequently than we need to talk. Such is the classical definition of prayer which is found among all the great masters of the spiritual life : Saint Francis de Sales, Saint Vincent de Paul, Saint Alphonsus Liguori, Saint Teresa. We should open up our hearts to Him as we would open the thurible, and send up, " as incense in His sight "[6] the perfume of our faith and adoration, of our trust and our contrition, of supplication and desire, and of the offering of ourselves. When we are tired of doing that, if one could grow tired of it, we should ask Him to speak to us . . . " Speak, Lord, for thy servant heareth."[7] Then Jesus will speak to us with the voice of God, of our Friend, of our Brother and our Spouse. We shall hear the inner voice of the Word assuming all

---

[6] Ps. 140, 2.
[7] I Kings iii, 9.

tones and giving us in turn strength, encouragement, reproach and above all, filling us with prayerfulness ; the divine voice to which we shall lend a docile ear and a willing heart. Thus shall we realise the true formula of prayer, meditation on Christ, with Christ and for Christ.

The purpose of prayer is to unite us more closely with God by a renewal and reinforcement of our love and meditation is the flame which renews the smouldering embers.

CHAPTER 15

THE MASS

IT is apparent at once that there is a harmonious and fruitful connection between the Mass and the imitation of Christ. The source of light and of love, the Mass is yet infinitely more for anyone who celebrates it or assists at its celebration. It is an incomparable act of imitation, being, as it is, the living reproduction of Jesus Crucified, and we shall never follow so closely in His footsteps as when we stand either on or at the foot of the altar. Meditation on the Sacrifice of the Mass, and it is important to meditate upon it before offering it, is a magnificent revelation to the soul of Christ's devotion to His heavenly Father and compassion for humanity.

While we study Christ in His entirety in order to endeavour to reproduce in our lives some of the wonders and mysteries and works of His, we must not lose sight of the fact that in His life there was one sovereign act, what one might call the act *par excellence* towards which His whole existence on this earth was oriented as towards its final goal and consummation ; the act which revolutionised heaven and earth and opened a new era in the history of the world, and that was His death. It is this death, freely accepted and transformed by religion and love into the sacrifice of adoration and redemption which has become by its mystical renewal and its continuity throughout the centuries the Holy Mass at which we can never assist without thinking on the Passion : " Do this for a commemoration of me."[1] To hear Mass with devotion we must recall that the sacrifice of the altar is exactly the same as that which was offered on Calvary. It is the quintessence of all the religion of Christ and of mankind ; an infinite sacrifice of adoration, benediction, expiation and prayer, offered by the Son for the glory of the Father. The Mass is the masterpiece of the eucharistic Heart of Jesus who loved us to the end, even to bloodshed and the " folly of the Cross."

---

[1] Luke xxii, 19.

If the Mass reveals the Heart of Jesus to us and stimulates our love for Him, it also calls for immolation on our part. It is our answer to this call which will be one of the greatest acts in our work of imitation, associating us intimately with the very sacrifice of Jesus Christ.   To the faithful and to the priest the words of Christ make the appeal : " Greater love than this no man hath, that a man lay down his life for his friends."[2]   To celebrate and assist at Mass is not only to offer Jesus Christ, but to offer oneself with and like Jesus Christ.   By Baptism and by Holy Orders we priests are united and incorporated in Jesus Christ, to such an extent that we are but one full Being, one in Christ.   Then Jesus the Priest is the victim of His own priesthood, the Priest and the Victim, and we too are priests and victims, the extension of the priesthood of Jesus Christ.   So all of us, in greater or lesser degree, become part of the " kingly priesthood."[3]

This is one of the most austere and perhaps least understood aspects of the holy sacrifice.   Yet, unless we understand and practice this immolation of ourselves, we shall not perfectly understand celebration of or assistance at Mass, which might properly be defined as a personal offering joined to that of Jesus Christ.   We should understand that it is *His* Mass, and that we are completing by it " those things that are wanting of the suffering of Christ "[4] and that we are dying with Him and like him for the glory of God and the salvation of souls.

Our first action at the altar is to place ourselves, as it were, on the paten and in the chalice ;   a tiny host by the side of the large one, a drop of water mixed with the wine which is going to become His Blood.   Then we offer ourselves to the Father, whole and entire, body and soul, senses and faculties, holding back nothing.   All is for God and at all times, and our offering is inspired by the deepest feelings of religion and of love, so that we wish to become His holocaust. Thus the Mass becomes an eminent act of devotion, if that could be called devotion in which there is something far more fundamental, namely a delivery of one's entire being

---

[2] John xv, 13.
[3] I Pet. II, 9.
[4] Coloss. i, 24.

to the worship and the service of God. This we realise when we consider that the Mass is the most important exercise of the spiritual life, the very centre and soul of all religion.

The first act then of the priest and of the faithful at the Mass is to offer ourselves in sacrifice to God, and the second is to *die*, not in the corporal sense, but to die a spiritual and mystical death like our Saviour. In other words, we endeavour to kill in ourselves all that is unworthy of God and of our vocation of victim, for God cannot accept any but pure and holy sacrifices. So we set about destroying all sin and the shadow of sin in ourselves ; the two great human passions of pride and sensualism, with all their varied offshoots, and all thoughts, desires and emotions, of will, of word and of action which would not bear the seal of religion and the mark of the victim. In a word, we destroy the old man.

When we die with Christ on the altar we accept patiently, joyfully and lovingly work, suffering, temptation, mortification, persecution, all the crosses which Providence may lay upon our shoulders. In all our tribulations, great or little, we profit by the Mass by saying with the love and obedience of Christ in Gethsemani, " not my will but thine." We develop in our souls the spirit of penance and of expiation, the spirit which desires suffering and martyrdom. When we die with Christ on the altar we envisage the sufferings of the day and go to meet them with open hearts and wills, uniting them to the sacrifice of Jesus on the altar. We accept in advance whatever death awaits us, at the place and time, and in the circumstances ordained by God, even as Jesus Christ accepted His death, and we transform it, as He did, into a supreme sacrifice for the glorification of the Holy Trinity and the redemption of the world, the triumphant death of the Christian and the priest.

Offered now and slain on the altar, the Host has still to be consumed. This consummation of the sacrifice of the Mass in ourselves is achieved in Communion and by love. Communion is the mystical death of our own personality, for by Communion our personality is purified, elevated and sanctified to the point where it changes entirely. In Communion we cease to live our fleshly lives and live in Jesus Christ. We cease to be poor men and become like gods, other Christs. Though it is we who consume Christ, it is really He who consumes us, and assimilates us into His own Being. Even if we cannot receive Holy Communion the consummation of our personal sacrifice may be achieved by love.

In former days the holocaust used to be consumed by fire. The fire of the new sacrifice, which devours the spiritual Victim who is Christ, and such as we are, ourselves, is love. The essential act of anyone who celebrates or assists at Mass is to be consumed by love for God, for Christ and for His Church. We must, in imitation of and in union with Christ adore and bless God, ask pardon, implore mercy, but above all, we must love Him. None of these acts has great value or bears much fruit unless inspired and divinised by love.

CHAPTER 16

HOLY COMMUNION

THE Holy Eucharist is at one and the same time a sacrifice and a sacrament. We have seen how we may imitate Christ by the celebration of or assistance at the sacrifice of the Mass and we shall now show how we can attain to an even more remarkable and indeed triumphant imitation through the sacrament of Holy Communion.

The consumed Host enters into our being imprinting upon it the divine likeness, like a seal pressed on melted wax. Incorporated thus in Christ, sharing His perfections and His life, nothing could be more natural than that we should act thereafter with Him and like Him, and so achieve our aim of imitation. The influence of the Blessed Sacrament, however, is always conditioned by the perfection of our preparation for and our reception of it, and the action of grace in our souls. For the disciple of Jesus Christ there is a right and fruitful way of going to receive Holy Communion.

Christ Himself is the original agent of our sanctification, and our role consists in yielding to His action and co-operating with Him in the capacity of an instrument in the work. Every day, and a hundred times a day He takes us up and works on us, through the Holy Ghost or through the action of His grace, from a distance ; but in Holy Communion, being actually and personally in us, He reaches us directly and can mould and shape us with His own divine hands. Christ is never so close to us, so active in us, as at that moment when He comes into direct contact with our poor humanity and thus raises it, as the leaven the dough.

Holy Communion is the supreme effort of the love of Christ to give Himself to us, to unite and identify us with Himself. Anyone who carries Jesus Christ within him cannot help but reflect His nature and His life. All the more then, we must repeat, is it necessary that this marvellous work of the Master should discover in us the right measure of preparation and welcome? If we wish our Lord to fashion us after His own likeness, that is as a host or victim, then let us make sure that we offer to Him a soul of pure unleavened bread.   If we desire the divine artist to sculpt His own likeness from the block of our being, let us ensure that the block is of the finest extraction and excellent grain.

To achieve this we first of all intensify the work of our imitation.   If we live from morning to night in the loving presence of Jesus Christ, compelled by His example to practise purity, obedience, poverty, humility, recollection, abnegation ; if all the time and everywhere we endeavour to perform the will of God as expressed by the Holy Rule, by our superiors, by the duties of our station, and all for the glory of God and the salvation of the world, then we may worthily approach the Holy Table.   If we are clothed in Christ, then indeed we wear the wedding gown and may partake of the feast.   At the sight of the communicant who resembles Him Christ is filled with joy, and unites Himself with him in the same way as a mother recognising the likeness to herself in her little one hugs him to her heart and nurtures him tenderly.

To this general preparation let us now add another and more immediate one, filled with love.   Jesus the Host comes to us with His whole Heart ; with all our hearts let us go out to meet Him.   Let our communions be filled with love and the desire to gratify and console the Heart of Jesus.   One of His sweetest joys in the morning meeting with us is the exchange of gifts.   Without such preparation Holy Communion can be fraught with semi-sterility, for union with and resemblance to Christ cannot effectively take place but in and through love.

The big obstacle to the action of the Holy Eucharist is the want of perfection.   Jesus the spotless Host loves to descend only into consciences as white as the corporal and hearts as pure and clean as the ciborium.   At the Last Supper He Himself washed the dusty feet of His Apostles.   Consequently the communicant must take care to renew moral virginity in his soul.   Baptism of fire, which is love, effaces all spiritual stain and consumes all moral dross.   " He shall baptise you with the Holy Ghost and with fire." [1]

---

[1] Luke iii, 16.

We must not, however, lose sight of the fact that neither preparation for Holy Communion nor the action of grace in the soul are, for all their importance, Holy Communion. They only ensure for the soul which wishes to reproduce Christ the greatest reward for its effort. The communicant is both active and passive. He is passive beneath the hand of Christ which moulds him, and active through his own interior reaction. As the clay which is pounded and whisked assumes the shape of the vase into which it is cast, so the soul absorbed and moulded by Christ endeavours to adjust itself to Him and to conform to His wishes, and that is the action of grace.

Holy Communion is a dual undertaking ; on the part of the soul towards Christ, and on the part of Christ towards the soul. He possesses us, we possess Him ; He consumes us, we consume Him ; He becomes part of us, we become part of Him. It is a spiritual undertaking for the communicant, involving faith, hope and charity, for the theological virtues alone possess the privilege of reaching God direct and there the communicant finds the nourishment for his soul.

The first act after receiving Holy Communion will be an act of adoring faith in the real and personal presence of Jesus Christ in us ; a profound and prolonged act of faith, for by thus plunging the soul into an atmosphere of sustained and intense recollection we are laying the foundation for the action of all the graces therein. Faith leads to hope. We believe in Jesus the Host, and we hope in Him. We trust in His power, we confide ourselves to His generosity, we abandon ourselves to His embrace as would a child to his mother. Faith and hope are but a prelude to that union which as we have seen is consummated in love. The act of charity is the centre which draws all graces towards it. We love Jesus, we tell Him of our love and we desire to be with Him for ever. Among the variety of acts of love which we now make, we should choose for preference those which unite us most closely with Him ; acts of tenderness, of conformity with His will, of self-abandonment. We shall find then that we are really participating in the abundance of Christ's virtues and perfections, and approaching a much closer realisation of the ideal of sanctity.

Union with our divine Saviour calls for action with Him, a co-operation with His work which will result in our becoming more like Him all the time. Christ, consumed in Holy Communion, lives in us in His capacity of victim ; He does not die, but remains a living and active personality. Christ the Host is both priest and victim as we have seen, and He continues in our hearts the essential work of His priesthood, the sacrifice of Himself for the glorification of God and the salvation of the world. We now associate ourselves with His sacerdotal work, by offering ourselves with Him and like Him, as a holocaust, and thus Holy Communion the sacrament becomes Holy Communion the sacrifice. Now that we have become part of the mystical Christ, joined to Christ the Priest, members of His priesthood, we fulfil our priestly duties with Him and through Him, and thus we prolong and consummate the sacrifice of the Mass.

As we now bear the Host within us, our first religious gesture will be to offer to God in sacrifice Jesus present in us, His Body, His Blood, His Soul, His Divinity, His Passion, Agony and Death. Our second and sacerdotal gesture will be to offer and immolate ourselves always in union with Jesus Christ, as in the Mass, with love and through love.

With Jesus Christ, and like Him and through Him we prostrate ourselves before the Holy Trinity and render to It in the name of the Church and of mankind the homage of our adoration, humility, submission and praise. We offer thanks for the wonderful blessings of the Creation, the Incarnation, the Redemption, for all the graces accorded to the Sacred Humanity of Jesus and the soul of the Blessed Virgin, and above all for the graces accorded to ourselves and in particular for calling us to be Christians, religious or priests. We ask pardon for all the sins committed through the centuries and we pray, a powerful and divine prayer, through Christ and with Him, which is always heard.

We commence our prayer with attention to God and to His interests. From the depths of our hearts we address our three requests to the Father : Our Father who art in heaven, hallowed be thy name, thy kingdom come, thy will be done on earth as it is in heaven. We follow this with prayer for all humanity. In company with Christ we mention all human distress and ask for the conversion of infidels and heretics, for sinners and for the perseverance of the just. We recommend to our heavenly Father the Church, the Pope, the bishops, the priests, the religious and all Christian souls, with special remembrance for our own spiritual father, our congregation, our community. We do not forget our parents, our superiors, our subjects, our brethren, our friends, our benefactors, even our enemies. We make final mention of the souls in Purgatory. Finally let us pray for ourselves, that we may obtain all the graces attendant upon imitation. Of this prayer we shall speak more fully in a later chapter, when we come to the second rule of our method of sanctification and its application.

This method of using the graces of the Mass and Holy Communion is the most truly Christian and theological : Christian because it embodies the most essential elements of religion and holiness, namely, faith, hope, charity, devotion sacrifice, adoration ; theological because it is the logical application of the doctrinal teaching we have received on the purpose and power of the Holy Eucharist, sacrament and sacrifice.

CHAPTER 17

THE DIVINE OFFICE—THE ROSARY—THE WAY OF THE CROSS

IN the various spiritual exercises which we perform, and in particular in the recitation of the Divine Office, we can discover a most rewarding method of applying ourselves to a loving and imitative contemplation of Jesus Christ. To accord to this wonderful prayer a purely routine and rapid recitation, to make of it, as Saint Teresa said, a sort of " sad music," is to commence with many faults and conclude with little profit. The priest who is desirous of imitating Christ will endeavour to make of it a perfect prayer, on Christ, with Christ and like Christ. For the Divine Office must be a prayer of the heart as well as of the lips. In the preparatory prayer we are asked to bring to its recitation a devout soul, and devotion implies an intellectual and zealous reflection upon God and above all upon Jesus Christ. To think about our Redeemer while saying the Office, to meditate on His life and contemplate His virtues is rewarding and delightful, especially if we make full use of the psalms to enrich and increase our knowledge and our thought. For the psalms are full of Him. At every turn we see in the light of their prophecies the adorable form of Jesus. The Psalter in particular, says Cardinal Mercier, on every one of its pages interprets for us the soul of Jesus.

The Liturgy too is a precious mine to be exploited. As we have already seen, each feast of the Church offers a new revelation of the life and mysteries of Christ. So while reciting the psalms we can enter into the liturgical spirit of the day, and find yet again another source of meditation upon Jesus our Model. Such prayer can be used without hesitation as or in the place of prayer on the Passion. It was from it that the Curé of Ars derived his heroic passion for sacrifice. But it is even more effective if we recite the Divine Office in company with Jesus Christ Himself. Liturgical prayer is not an individual thing ; it is the public official prayer of the Church, the prayer of Christ, and we shall do better to give our voices over to Him, so that it will be He who prays through us, then we shall pray with Him : two prayers which are but one.

Finally let us make of the Divine Office a spiritual sacrifice by reciting it with the same intention as our Saviour, that is, the glory of God and the salvation of the world. " Offer to God the sacrifice of praise : and pay vows to the most High,"[1] and the " sacrifice of praise shall glorify "[2] Him, so that our " prayer be directed as incense in His sight."[3] It is the prayer of faith, hope and charity, the prayer of adoration and benediction, of pardon and supplication, the prayer of glorification and salvation.

Method of Reciting the Divine Office

1. *Before the Office :* Let us unite ourselves intimately with the spirit and heart of Jesus Christ, by an inward act of contemplation, so that we may pray with Him for His intentions : the glory of the Father and the salvation of the world.

2. *During the Office :* Let us study the Psalmody with reference to Christ, the Church, ourselves and all members of the Mystical Body of Christ ; or let us meditate on the " christological " mystery of the feast ; or let us contemplate tenderly the scenes of the Passion.

3. *At the commencement* of each nocturne and the different hours, let us renew briefly and fervently our intention to recite the Office with Jesus and like Jesus in a spirit of religion and apostolic zeal.

★   ★   ★   ★   ★   ★   ★

The Rosary

Everyone says the Rosary in honour of the Blessed Virgin. The Liturgy has consecrated a special feast and Catholic piety has set aside a special month dedicated to it. For thousands and

---

[1] Ps. 49, 14.
[2] Ps. 49, 23.
[3] Ps. 140, 2.

thousands of Christian souls the Rosary is a source of joy and comfort and love. It goes with them even into the grave in their joined hands, as a pledge of immortal hope. So too this special Marian devotion can be harmonised excellently with our method of self-sanctification. There is, however, a danger which we may not always escape of allowing our recitation of it to become a monotonous and mechanical repetition of Ave Marias cut up regularly with a Pater and a Gloria, the mind wandering meanwhile and the imagination daydreaming. This will not do. The recitation of the Rosary is not really a prayer at all unless the sound made by the lips carries an intelligible meaning which is heard in the depths of the soul. As we pass the beads through our fingers we must meditate on their significance in our hearts. The only true meaning of the prayer of the Rosary and an essential for gaining its indulgence is the meditation on its mysteries.

The Rosary takes on the form of a prayer on our Lord and His Blessed Mother for its mysteries are filled with their presence, their actions and their holiness. There are dogmatic splendours and moral riches to be found in this gallery of living frescoes. To put it another way, the Rosary is like a precious vein that we must exploit if we wish to perfect our work of imitation. At the same time we want to avoid an unappetising monotony or over familiarity with its mysteries and so we suggest that in order to impart to it an air of freshness we should incorporate it within the framework of the programme we have attempted to lay down for imitating Christ. We could, for instance, during our contemplation of the scenes of the Gospel, dwell on Jesus and Mary as models of the special virtue of the month. This is an excellent habit to form, for with time and the grace of God it produces the very best results.

For example : October : Dedicated to Silence and Recollection. First Mystery : The Annunciation. The silent and interior recollection of the Blessed Virgin in this unique moment in the story of mankind. The future Mother of God, living far from the world, solitary in her little room in the Temple, plunged in deep contemplation. When the Holy Ghost overshadows her there is silence all around her, and above all in the depths of her enraptured soul: the silence of humility, of adoration and of love. The recollection of Jesus in the womb of His Blessed Mother, in His prison of the flesh . . .where He too lived alone and separated from the exterior world, but in the sight of God.

Second Mystery: The Visitation. Mary sets off in haste . . . leaving her customary surroundings . . . encountering all sorts of trivial and noisy people and places . . . she travels alone . . . with her Treasure . . . silent and always in an ecstasy of love . . . she goes direct . . . without stopping . . . seeing nothing . . . hearing nothing except the Heart of her Child which is beating close to her own . . . Jesus, the Word, always silent too. Here is the ideal of the missionary who brings Christ to souls.

Third Mystery: The Nativity. The mystery of recollection. The night . . . the lonely cave . . . far from the tumult of the teeming crowds . . . the silence of earth and heaven . . . everyone and everything asleep. *Dum medium silentium tenerent omnia.*[4] Jesus is born , . . not a cry, not a word. Just the faith, adoration and love of Mary and Joseph. Silence always accompanies the divine works.

Another Example: The Month of November. Prayer and Supplication

First Sorrowful Mystery: The Agony in the Garden. The vision of sin, and of the Passion. Horror and crushing agony. The prayer of Jesus : *filial,* Father, *imploring,* if it be possible, *resigned,* nevertheless not my will but thine be done. The constant and repeated prayer, all powerful ; " And there appeared to him an angel from heaven, strengthening him."[5] In physical suffering, in agonies of the soul let us imitate Jesus, let us pray, pray again, pray all the time. Let us ever remember His injunction : " Pray, lest you enter into temptation."[6]

Second Mystery: The Scourging at the Pillar. Jesus stripped and scourged like a slave. The martyrdom of the body, and of natural modesty. The Victim does not pray with

---

[4] Introit : Sunday within Octave of Nativity.
[5] Luke xxii, 43.
[6] Luke xxii, 40.

His lips, but continues His prayer within the soul. The silent offering of His blood in expiation of human luxury and for the purity of all His consecrated priests and religious. Let us imitate our Saviour : pray to remain chaste, pray for the victims of fleshly vice.

Fifth Mystery : The Crucifixion. The prayer of Jesus . . . His call to Heaven . . . " My God, my God why has thou forsaken me ? " The suppliant call of the soul thirsting for love. . . " I thirst . . . " His prayer for His executioners : " Father, forgive them, for they know not what they do " . . . The prayer of the Good Thief : " Lord, remember me when thou shalt come into thy kingdom " . . . Let us pray like Jesus Christ, with the Good Thief. Let us pray that the thirst of the Crucified may be quenched ; let us pray for the persecutors of the Church, for our enemies, and let us ask for mercy for ourselves.

★　　★　　★　　★　　★　　★　　★

The Way of the Cross

The Stations of the Cross is another Catholic devotion full of love, and a perfect exercise for imitation, general and particular. At each of the fourteen stations let us stop an instant and pray, always with our Lord. Let us contemplate Him with the sorrowing love of the imitator ; let us listen to Him and speak to Him. First let us listen to His words . . . to His words to Pilate, words of truth and of justice. . . . " Art thou a king then ? . . . Thou sayest that I am a king." Words of pity to the women of those who were going to execute Him . . . " Weep not over me ; but weep for yourselves and for your children." Words of love and infinite tenderness . . . " Behold thy son . . . Behold thy Mother." Words of mercy : " Father, forgive them for they know not what they do." Words of pardon and of hope to the penitent thief : " Amen I say to thee, this day thou shalt be with me in paradise." Words of suffering and desire : " I thirst." Words of filial abandonment : " Father, into thy hands I commend my spirit." Words of the supreme sacrifice of love : " It is consummated." Listen to Jesus Christ, to the powerful voice of His sufferings, passion and death. Listen to His prodigious silences : " But Jesus held his peace," a thousand times more eloquent and impressive than words themselves.

And let us talk to Him. Let us tell Him of our faith, our trust, our compassion, our repentance, our love. Let us assure Him of our resolution to love Him, to love Him more and more, as He loves us, " to the end . . . unto death, even to the death of the Cross " . . . to love Him with a fruitful love like His own rooted in the heroic virtues of obedience, humility, patience, the spirit of sacrifice, which are the virtues characteristic of our work of imitation.

The Way of the Cross is the life of the Christian, the religious, the priest, of which each day is a station. " If any man will come after me, let him deny himself, and take up his cross daily, and follow me."[7] Before we start upon our way of the cross let us travel with Christ along the road to Calvary and that will give us the heart to accept in advance and carry bravely all the hundred and one little crosses with which our lives are marked. We should also carefully pick out a special virtue and as we have shown with the Rosary give it our special attention as we make the Stations, contemplating Jesus Christ as the model of the particular virtue of the month.

For Example. October. Silence and Recollection.

The silence of Jesus during His Passion ; His silence before Herod and Pilate, before His accusers and executioners ; His silence during the storm of insults, calumnies and blasphemies ; His silence before the cross which He embraces, and before His mother when He meets her. " Jesus held his peace." If He speaks at all it is to pray, to console, to pardon, to assure the Father of His submission and His love ; the silence of death and the silence of the sepulchre. And all the time there is too the interior silence of Christ . . . profound, continuous, unalterable recollection . . . Shaken as by a hurricane of sufferings, He maintains a serenity which nothing can disturb . . . all the time united to the Father by thought, heart and will . . " Father . . . not as I will, but as

---

[7] Luke ix, 23.

thou wilt." What an example for us to contemplate and reproduce ! Every day of the month along our way of the cross we must have the determination to maintain like Christ a continual silence, in pain, separation, mourning, in humiliation, sickness and death ; a silence of submission, of strength and of love. We must know how to hold our peace with Christ and to speak only through the duty of charity. At hours of crisis we must learn to live in calm and peace, without reproach or revolt, and to draw from the thought of God and the sight of the Crucified the strength to suffer, and hold our peace, and love.

Another Example. May. Poverty.

" Blessed are the poor." We take now the virtue of poverty, the actual spirit of poverty which extends even to complete renunciation.

The poverty of Jesus, " abject, poor, rejected, scorned and totally necessitous," says Saint Francis de Sales. Deprived of the majesty which His Divinity should have accorded Him, deprived even of His dignity as a man, treated as a traitor, a slave and a fool . . . " a worm and no man." His separation from His Mother, their brief meeting before the final separation which was coming. His personal detachment and forgetfulness of self . . . " Weep not for me." . . .

Then there is His material poverty . . . For His bruised and bleeding face He has nothing . . . He is dependent on someone who will bathe it in the towel . . . for His parched throat someone else gives Him a drink of vinegar . . . there is nothing to wrap His body in until someone provides a winding sheet . . . there is nowhere to lay Him until He is given a tomb. The very clothes He is wearing at His death are snatched from Him and drawn for in a lottery, so that now He has nothing even to cover His nakedness. He was poor at His birth, still poorer during His lifetime, and on the Cross, poorest of all.

In this complete denudation He still had His Father . . . and the ineffable sweetness of feeling Himself loved. And finally even this was too much for Him to have. It seemed as if the Father had withdrawn and was angry . . . and this final consolation, to which His agonised soul had clung, like the shipwrecked mariner to a plank, deserts Him, and

He is plunged into a gulf of desolation. " My God, my God, why has thou forsaken me ? "[8]

Holy poverty . . . ennobled by Jesus who died in its embrace. Before this magnificent revelation of poverty let us cry with Saint Francis of Assissi : " O most needy Jesus, the grace I ask of you is to give me the privilege of Poverty . . .Who would not love Lady Poverty above all the others ? "

---

[8] Mark xv. 34.

CHAPTER 18

INTIMACY WITH JESUS

AT prayer, at Mass, at Holy Communion, during the recital of the Divine Office, the Rosary and the Way of the Cross we can unite ourselves to Jesus Christ in loving contemplation, and by an interior act of imitation of Him. We will maintain this divine and rewarding contact throughout the day : " Stay with us, Lord," said the disciples on the road to Emmaus. Be our inseparable Companion on the journey. So that we may never lose our way, let us stimulate in ourselves a fresh interest in our habitual practices of recollection : the practice of the presence of God, good dispositions, ejaculatory prayers, visits to the Blessed Sacrament.

The presence of God is a fundamental and unshakable necessity in any attempt at an interior life. It ought to be a familiar concomitant of all our actions. If we are to become imitators of Jesus Christ, our practice will be to come as close as possible to the Man-God, Emmanuel, the Second Person of the Blessed Trinity, and to live constantly in the light of recollection of Him. We ought to be able to feel that we can almost see Him, that we can sense Him close to us, as inseparable as our shadows. The first way to practise the presence of God is to imagine to ourselves that our Saviour accompanies us everywhere, and that we can see Him in every place. After that, and best of all, we shall find Him in the temple of our souls, where He resides in company with the Father and the Holy Ghost. " If anyone love me . . . my Father will love him, and we will come to him and will make our abode with him."[1] The whole secret is to live constantly in sensible apprehension of His presence.

So we return unceasingly to the thought of, and the love of Jesus, for it is impossible to think on Him without increasing our love. We can profit by this return to the thought of Christ at the start or during the course of our various occupa-

[1] John xiv, 23.

tions, to renew our good dispositions, our intention to work and to suffer in order to please and console the Heart of Jesus. *All for Jesus* is the title of one of Father Faber's works, and it is a most suitable motto for our lives. To please Jesus is the formula for a good disposition which is found constantly in the writings of Saint Alphonsus, in his ascetic writings, in his directions circulated to his Congregation and in the primitive Rule.

Let us cultivate more assiduously and ardently our devotion to the act of love, for every thought on Jesus Christ expands into greater love of Him. Twenty, thirty, a hundred times a day, during prayer, or Holy Communion, during a visit, while reading, in the cell or the refectory, walking, everywhere and at all times, in an abundance of love let us multiply our ejaculatory prayers in the form of affective aspirations to our Lord : " Jesus I love You : O Christ, mercy and pardon. It is You whom I desire. Jesus my love, may Your will be accomplished." Let us thus sow in our lives fruitful seeds of love which will return a rich harvest.

Another excellent manner of realising a habitual and loving recollection of Jesus Christ is by visits to the Blessed Sacrament. Outside of the official and obligatory visit which obtains in most religious orders, be on the look-out also for all sorts of occasions ; if necessary, make opportunities, for example the recitation of the Office, entering or leaving the monastery, passing a church or oratory, for going to greet our great Friend who waits all the time for us in the tabernacle. Such little visits made for sheer love are more likely than anyone could believe to stir the fires of our interior life and to deepen our intimacy with Jesus Christ. Nor should we forget the spiritual visit to the Blessed Sacrament. Thought knows no distances nor are walls barriers to the union of hearts. From time to time, when we are a long way from His presence in the Blessed Sacrament, or at night if we awaken, we can send our thoughts to Him, and turn our souls towards Him in a desire for communion with Him. That way Christ will become the axis of our spiritual lives and this is His proper place in the lives of His imitators.

There remains just one important thing to say on the

subject of the intellectual life of the priest or religious, and
its place and rôle in our method of self-sanctification. To
conceive of the intellectual life as something apart from the
imitation of Christ, separated from it as if it were in a water-
tight compartment would not only be a mistake, but a fault.
It is impossible to imagine life as a series of pigeon holes or
drawers all independent of each other. Life is a highly
organised hierarchy of all our faculties, members and functions,
interdependent upon one another in their activity and development. Obviously then intellectual work must have its
own repercussions for good or bad upon the spirituality of
each.

In our century perhaps more necessarily than ever it is
important for the religious or the priest to have a predilec-
tion for scriptural, theological or ascetical writing treating
especially of the person of Jesus Christ ; yet he must at the
same time avoid a narrow or exclusive approach to the
organisation of study. Before an enormous mass of writings,
ancient and modern, we are faced with a choice. We must
reject the bad, the insignificant, the mediocre, even the good,
and keep only the excellent and outstanding works in our
libraries. A work is excellent if it contributes efficaciously
to the work of our sanctification and of our apostolate. Saint
Benedict counselled his monks to choose, among the works
of the Fathers, those which conduced most to the greatest
perfection. Now the highest perfection is synonymous
with the most perfect imitation of Jesus Christ. For the
religious or the priest, study is not an end in itself, it is purely
a means towards zeal and sanctity. It is this point of view
that the apostle, conscious of his vocation, places before
himself in appraising the value of a work and in making
his choice. Above all, seek the true knowledge, the divine
knowledge, which is that of Christ.

The foundation stone of our study should be the Bible,
and in the Bible let us dwell longest and return most frequently
to the Gospels, the Epistles of Saint Paul and the Psalms,
for all of these are full of the Redeemer. To read these
and to meditate upon them is to commune spiritually with
Jesus, and to refresh ourselves with a nourishment whose
flavour is that of the Host. When we are at home, that is

apart from mission work, at least, let us make sure that we do not pass a day without such communion.

Amongst all the immense religious bibliography, we should go by instinct towards the " christological " writings of the Fathers, the saints and the theologians. This is a study which we can continue lovingly all our lives, so that we may make of our souls a veritable library of Jesus Christ. Such a wide and deep study of Jesus Christ becomes a wonderful instrument of sanctification and a powerful weapon in our apostolate. Filled to overflowing with Him ourselves we can pour Him out over souls. Far from degenerating then into a cold abstract instruction, our preaching will blaze with the warmth of charity and appeal to all hearts. We shall preach only Christ crucified. Whether we are orators will not matter, but we shall certainly become apostles. The active life of the missioner will then be a flowering of his contemplative life. The text of Saint Thomas to the Order of Preachers will be realised again in him . . . namely to contemplate and to give to souls the fruit of his contemplation. And far from being an obstacle to his interior life his apostolate will help and sustain him in developing it.

Assuming now that each morning a soul who wishes to imitate Christ is girding himself for this programme, orientating his *interior* life towards Christ : prayers, the Mass, Communion, the Breviary, the Rosary, the Way of the Cross ; his life of *recollection* : the practice of the presence of God, good intentions, ejaculatory prayers, visits to the Blessed Sacrament ; the greater part of his *intellectual* life : reading, study ; we may say that such a soul by thus acquiring our proposed universal, profound, loving and actual knowledge of our Saviour is conforming to the basic law of our method of imitation. In these conditions imitation of Jesus Christ will appear not as an unattainable lure but as a splendid and realisable practical programme, and it will not be to this religious that our Saviour can say, as He said to the Apostle Philip : " Have I been so long a time with you and have you not known me ? " [2]

---

[2] John xiv, 9.

CHAPTER 19

THE GREAT LAW

"THE great medium of prayer" would be a suitable title for this chapter. For anyone who aims to reproduce Christ prayer is obviously the principal, universal and essential medium. It is the fundamental law of all spiritual life and of the particular method of sanctification recommended here. *The imitation of Christ is an outstanding grace which can only be obtained by perfect and continual prayer.* It is clear that this necessity for prayer is simply a logical and particular application of a universal law proclaimed throughout the Gospels, for example : " We ought always to pray"[1] and " Pray without ceasing."[2] If prayer is thus an indispensable requirement for the leading of the ordinary Christian life which implies a general but more or less loose imitation of Jesus Christ, it is clearly the first demand on the person who is setting out on the work of self-sanctification by precise and perfect imitation of our Redeemer.

Imitation is the virtue of virtues and the grace of graces. It is a leading grace which summarises and contains all the others. The " christification " of our souls and lives is essentially a supernatural work and surely the most sublime supernatural task is this ascent of our whole being towards Christ and in Christ, ending in union, almost in identification with Him. It is a second creation which surpasses the first in beauty and richness ; another incarnation, a mystical extension and development of the Incarnation of Christ in the womb of the Blessed Virgin. Quite evidently this is something which is above and beyond our poor human powers. It is a tremendous work requiring tremendous grace, which in its turn demands prodigious prayer based upon invincible faith, profound humility and filial trust.

Imitation is a great and continuous work, involving all our days and every minute of them, without interruption

[1] Luke xviii, 1.
[2] Thess. v, 17.

92

or pause. So it is apparent that such ceaseless activity requires a continual flow of actual grace to our souls : " Without me you can do nothing."[3] At the back of any supernatural work we can distinguish always divine intervention and the presence of grace. Imitation, grace, prayer : these are three links in the same chain, which are indissolubly interwoven. Prayer attracts grace, which in its turn primes and supports our spiritual work. While on the contrary, all weakening in prayer results immediately and inevitably in a restriction of grace and thence in a lessening of imitation. Continual imitation, continual grace, continual prayer : thus and only thus is the conquest of sanctity possible, by an incessant supplication which will mobilise to our rescue all the graces of heaven.

We need too the grace of illumination, that we may better understand the sublimity and realise the necessity for our method of self-sanctification, and that we may develop our deep and loving knowledge of Jesus Christ. Such knowledge is much more the result of divine light than of our theological studies : " No one knoweth . . . who the Father is, but the Son, and to whom the Son will reveal him."[4] " Neither is it flesh or blood which will reveal Jesus Christ but the Father who is in heaven."[5] It was Saint Paul who on his knees asked God to enlighten the Ephesians so that they might be able to " comprehend what is the breadth, and length, and height, and depth : to know also the charity of Christ, which surpasseth all knowledge."[6]

There is a special grace of enlightenment which turns the interior life towards intuitive recollection so that we begin to live continuously in the presence of Christ. Our Lord is the true light, and it is in this light and by means of this light that we shall be enriched with a full " understanding, unto the knowledge of the mystery of God the Father and of Christ Jesus : in whom are hid all the treasures of wisdom and knowledge."[7]

---

[3] John xv, 5.
[4] Luke x, 22.
[5] Matt. xvi, 17.
[6] Eph. iii, 14, 19.
[7] Coloss. ii, 2-3.

There is the grace of love, in its highest and purest form, the friendship of Jesus Christ. The friendship of Christ is the supreme gift and the communication of the Holy Ghost, called down by the cry from our hearts : " the charity of God is poured forth in our hearts, by the Holy Ghost, who is given to us."[8]

There are also : the grace of all the virtues : chastity, humility, obedience, poverty, since we shall be imitating all the virtues of Christ and the practice of these virtues is conditioned always by supernatural grace ; and the grace of strength : our imitation in the character of victims demands a complete mastery of self, and the instant suppression of all thrusts of egoism, the exercise of total self-abnegation, the love of the Cross and the spirit of sacrifice ; and for all that magnanimity, generosity, even heroism are required.

Finally there is the grace of perseverance, for imitation is not the work of a day, but the work of every day, the uninterrupted labour of a lifetime, without rest or discouragement. But all these extraordinary graces are the fruit only of extraordinary prayer : extraordinary that is by its perfection and its continuity. The ideal, and we shall see later how to attain it, is to orientate all our prayers towards the imitation of Jesus Christ, and to ask only that grace, which contains and sums up all the others. When we pray we are all God's beggars, and we remain at the door of the Father of the family, prostrate, imploring something . . . and that something is no less than God Himself. A beggar asks for bread and this is what we ask of God since Christ Himself said : " I am the living bread which comes down from heaven."[9]

So it is Christ, Christ only, that we may know Him, love Him and imitate Him, who is the exclusive object of our prayers. We may ask ourselves if any relative slackening in our reproduction of Christ in spite of good will may not spring chiefly from a neglect, more or less, and often unconscious, of this fundamental law of prayer. We must realise the literal significance of our Lord's words : " No man can come to me, except the Father, who hath sent me, draw

[8] Rom. v, 5.
[9] John vi, 51.

him."[10]   So we ask for the graces of imitation especially from Jesus Christ, the Holy Ghost and the Blessed Virgin, those three great architects of our sanctification, the same three architects of the mighty work of the Incarnation and the Redemption.

---

[10] John vi, 44.

CHAPTER 20

PRAYER TO CHRIST

IT was our Lord who first outlined the plan for the sanctification of souls, and therefore it is clear that it is to Him we must go first for help in putting His plan into operation. From whatever aspect we consider the work of imitation of Christ, we find that its moving principle is Jesus Christ, the Word Incarnate. He is our model in His life, passion, death and resurrection ; our strength and sustenance through the Holy Eucharist which incorporates us in Him, the living members of His Mystical Body. He is the true light by means of which we can follow Him and walk in His footsteps. He is the plenitude of all graces " of whose fulness we have all received," the origin and the end, the alpha and omega, the unique and necessary way. " No man cometh to the Father but by me."[2] Through Christ only can we hope to reach Christ : *Ad Jesum per Jesum.* Only by being grafted on to His life like the branch on to the vine, shall we be able to participate in His life and holiness, and come to resemble Him. He is the universal and permanent sacrament of our sanctification. All the radiance of the spiritual life comes from its natural centre in Him : He lives in us, but as to live is to act, the action of Christ in us is to assimilate us and transform us into the likeness of Himself and to cause us to live and act as He does.

Hence we need to develop the habit of prayer to our Saviour, imploring Him without ceasing to come and be born, to grow and to expand in our souls " unto the measure of the age of his fulness "[3] and to infuse into us, as the mother to the child in her womb all life, His life, His spirit, His love, His virtues, His interior dispositions, and by so doing, to render us in His own image. It is by praying to Christ and by living in Him that we shall live like Him : *per Dominum nostrum Jesum Christum.*

---

[1] John i, 16.
[2] John xiv, 6.   [3] Eph. iv, 13.

96

The work of Jesus Christ throughout the centuries—and it is the final proof of the divine origin of His Church in which He lives and of the sacraments through which He works—has consisted in raising humanity to Himself in order to regenerate and sanctify it. His is the divine leaven cast into the souls of men which turns them into bread, good bread, the Bread of Life. Let us repeat, however, that before Jesus Christ will thus come into our souls and change them we must ask Him to do so. Hence the vital importance of the cult of the Redeemer, of special devotion to His Incarnation, to His Passion, to the Holy Eucharist, to the Sacred Heart ; devotion which has no other purpose but to bring us to live in the atmosphere of Jesus Christ and to keep us there by faith, love and prayer in permanent contact with Him, and so to conduce us to a final perfect imitation of Him.

The exercises of piety, the practice of recollection, reading and study all veer us towards Christ, whom we have found, whom we have been given time to contemplate and to love, and whom we shall never leave. " I found him whom my soul loveth : I held him and I will not let him go."[4] When we reach Him in this manner we embark on a life of contemplation, of love and of prayer. Such intimacy with Jesus naturally stimulates the soul to the need for prayer, prayer to Christ Himself, constant and all-pervading. It is not sufficient to see and to delight in the Master, to listen to Him and to aspire to love Him more. It is necessary to pray to Him unceasingly, to ask Him to let us know Him better, to love Him more profoundly, to follow Him more closely. The toddler who is trying out his first steps holds tightly to his father's hand for fear of falling. On the steep and rugged path of imitation let us lean on Christ through prayer at every instant and step of the way. The grace of imitation like that of devotion is such that we ought " to ask for it longingly, to wait for it patiently and confidently, to receive it thankfully, to keep it humbly, to work with it diligently," says à Kempis.[5]

The opportunity to make the request to our Divine Lord for this leading grace to imitate Him will arise again and

---

[4] Cant. iii, 4.
[5] *Imit.* Bk. 4. ch. 15.

again, more or less explicitly in our daily pious exercises and meditation. In the morning, at the very start of prayer if possible, we make a brief survey of the moving principle of our life and remind ourselves of the fundamental spirit of our vocation ; then we may address a short and fervent prayer to our Redeemer to consecrate the day which is just starting and ask Him to make of it a perfect work of imitation. During the period allotted to prayer we shall make a special point of our appeal to Christ. Such an appeal according to Saint Alphonsus is not only an integral part of prayer, it is its very framework and final purpose. We pray in order to petition for grace, and our intimate and familiar colloquy with our Friend quite naturally takes on the shape of such petitions. Reflections, affections, resolutions are woven into a chain of prayer which contains all our supplication for the graces to imitate and resemble ever more closely Jesus our Model, contemplated, adored and loved.

We will ask Him to speak to us, to illuminate our hearts, to reveal Himself to us : " Speak, lord, for thy servant heareth." " Make thy face to shine upon thy servant."[6] From the Heart burning with love for us, the fountain of charity, we will ask the gift of genuine, total and generous love : Make our hearts like unto Thine. We will beg of Him to awaken great desires in our hearts, to raise us up towards Himself, to infuse into us something of His humility, chastity, obedience, poverty and recollection ; of His zeal for souls, and spirit of religion ; to give to our lives by reason of a clarity of vision like unto His, an irresistible impetus towards God. We will offer our resolutions then, the general resolution to imitate our Lord everywhere and at all times by a complete and loving conformity to the will of the Father, and the particular resolution to practise the virtue of the month, and to our resolutions we will add an urgent appeal for help, for without Him we can do nothing. This, then, is the prayer of the true imitator of Christ : eager and suppliant contemplation of Jesus our Model, with the object of reproducing Him in the soul.

Commencing with mental prayer this supplication extends throughout Mass and Holy Communion. The sacrifice of

---

[6] Ps. 118, 135.

the altar pervades the liturgy, and, bearing as it does, the
odour of the victim, it carries up also, the fragrance of supplication. Jesus the Victim pleads for us. As we have
already said, there is nothing better for all who are saying
or assisting at Mass than to unite themselves to Him in this
two-fold sacerdotal act. By Him, through Him and like
Him we offer Him and ourselves, the victims of love, for
the glory of God and the salvation of the world. By Him,
through Him and like Him, we pray. Occupied thus with
the glory of the Father and the fate of souls, let us be sure
not to forget ourselves, but to implore here again all the
graces and especially the most perfect of them all, that or
imitation. Let us ask Jesus Christ to allow us to travel with
Him on the road to Calvary. Let us beg of Him the grace
of abundant participation in His spirit of sacrifice, which is
the crowning joy of our work of imitation ; the grace to
understand, as He does, the meaning of the Cross, of loving
it and accepting it with patience, of seeking it generously
and of making of each day as it comes one continual Mass.

This prayer will occupy all our thanksgiving. One of our
greatest stumbling-blocks is not that we cannot pray, but
that we do not know what we should ask. We are like
professional beggars who do not know how to hold out
our hands. How opportune, indeed, was the cry of the
Apostles : " Lord, teach us to pray." [7]

We do not know how to pray except at Mass and Holy
Communion where Someone prays with us and for us,
Someone who is the incarnation of Prayer. Christ, whom
we have consumed at Holy Communion, is not dead but
alive and on the altars of our hearts. He is offering Himself,
a sacrificial victim of supplication. All we have to do is to
unite our entreaties to His, for we are no longer praying
on our own. There is a blending of two beings, two loves
and two prayers, which melt into one, our own prayer
being enveloped, absorbed and sanctified by that of Christ.
When we utter our prayer it passes through the Heart of
our Lord, from whence it emerges wholly pure and wholly
powerful. Pray to Jesus Christ, then, and using the formula
which concludes all the prayers of the Mass, *per Dominum*

---

[7] Luke xi, 1.

nostrum Jesum Christum, pray through Jesus Christ. Plead with the Father in the name of Jesus, for He will obtain us all things that the Father may be glorified in the Son.

The supplication at Mass and Holy Communion is complemented by the Divine Office. The Breviary beside being a song of praise, adoration and benediction, a canticle of faith, hope and charity, is also a petition. It is the prayer of Christ, of the Church and of the individual priest, and while maintaining all the time its character of universality, is by no means intended to exclude the voice of the soul which is endeavouring to attain to personal sanctity. As we meet Jesus, sorrowful or triumphant, then, on each page of the Divine Office, let us ask Him for the same portion of our daily bread, namely the grace to imitate Him perfectly throughout the day. Why ask anything else when this contains everything we want ? We make the same request in the main during the Way of the Cross. Each station is a miniature source of prayer, and as all prayer contains supplication, we shall ask of Christ suffering, fourteen times, the strength to follow Him on this royal road. Recalling our attention to specific imitation, we will ask also the grace to follow His example in practising the particular virtue of the month.

After thus recurring throughout our principal religious exercises, this petition to Christ overflows now into our interior life to sustain and perfect it ; for the interior life mingles in part at least with the life of prayer. When we speak of the life of prayer, we are speaking too of the life of supplication, for such petitions should flow continually through our daily lives, irrigating them with grace. The habitual presence of our Lord, the renewal of our good intentions, as many acts of love as we can make, frequent visits to the Blessed Sacrament, spiritual and corporal, are all ways of drawing prayer and supplication from the soul even as the morning sun in springtime invites the lark to soar and sing his jubilant song. The recollected soul living as it does in the loving company of Jesus will find a hundred ways during the day of asking his help and imitating Him. A troublesome or infuriating order : " O Jesus, help me to obey you . . . even unto death." A sudden humiliation : " O Thou who were gentle and humble of heart, teach me gentle-

ness and humility." A startling piece of bad news : " O
Master, give me the grace to repeat with You, ' Thy will be
done '." A calumny : " Lord, give me the strength to
forgive and forget." A temptation contrary to faith, or a
sudden violent attack of impure thoughts : " Lord save us
or we perish." A confining or irritating point of the Rule :
" O Jesus, help me by Your example to fulfil every ' jot and
tittle ' of the law." There are dozens of other supplications,
brief as a cry and swift as an arrow, with which we can fill in
odd moments. There are prayers inspired by the Holy
Ghost, or others which are the product of pious practices,
and amongst them we strongly recommend an invocation
to the Sacred Heart, to be renewed at the start of all our
actions, and every quarter of an hour or so : " Heart of Jesus,
example of *humility* or *poverty* (whatever the virtue of the
month happens to be) make my heart like unto Thine."

Even our intellectual life ought to be quickened by such
prayer. An imitator of Christ does not read from the stand-
point of the dilettante, but as a religious or a priest, not as
a scholar but as an apostle. Knowledge is not an end in
itself, but merely a means. Study should be always supernatural in its principal objective, namely to arrive at the
eternal truths and at a deeper knowledge of Jesus Christ,
and also in its ultimate purpose, that is the glory of God,
personal sanctity and the salvation of souls. Finally study
should be supernatural in itself, that is to say it should be
commenced, accompanied and terminated by prayer. Saint
Thomas did not begin a single article of the *Summa* without
prolonged entreaty, and he avowed that it was this which
provided the answer to the majority of the difficult objections.
In the manuscript of the *Summa, Against the Gentiles* are to
be seen scattered here and there amongst the most lofty
speculations the words *ave, ave, ave Maria.* Pascal always
went down on his knees and prayed before he started to
write. Saint Alphonsus composed his wonderful works
at the foot of the crucifix which he frequently kissed, and
before a statue of the Blessed Virgin, whom he constantly
invoked.

Let us then imitate the humility of the saints and the wisdom
of the doctors of the Church. In the matter of scientific,

theological or ascetical writings, or sermons, let us lean on Christ. He is the Truth, the Light which enlighteneth every man that cometh into this world, the Master of masters. In the doubts, difficulties and barren patches which our souls encounter, let us call : " Lord, illumine my shadows"[8] Let us entreat and the Spirit of Wisdom will descend on us and will give us the true knowledge,[9] not the knowledge which in Saint Paul's words puffs up but which edifies.[10] Above all let us so ask when we wish to scrutinise the depths of His holiness and the abyss of His divinity, for no one can know this except those to whom the Father wishes to reveal it,[11] that is to the " little ones " who have humbled themselves and asked.

To keep one's intellectual work in isolation from Christ is not only dangerous and foolish, but wrong. Let us entreat Christ during our studies too, that we may possess in greater and greater measure the truth which is in Him, and that we may like Him use it to sow the seeds of the glory of God and the salvation of the world.

It is hardly necessary to insist on the obvious tremendous power which such prayer to Jesus Christ, hourly prayer, accompanying and infiltrating through our entire moral and intellectual life, must have in obtaining graces for our work of imitation.

---

[8] Ps. 17, 29.
[9] Wisdom vii, 7, 17.
[10] I. Cor. viii, 1.
[11] Luke x, 22.

CHAPTER 21

CALL TO THE HOLY GHOST

CHRIST is the premier architect of our salvation, but He
is not the only one. His principal collaborator is the
Holy Ghost whose role in the life of our Redeemer
gives us some idea of His influence in ours.

It was through the Holy Ghost that the Word became flesh
and was made man. It was the Holy Ghost who led Jesus
into the desert, descended upon Him in the form of a dove,
guided Him through His apostolic journeys, was the active
power at His baptism and lived in Him, filling Christ with
His gifts.

In the Mystical Body of Christ we too share in the universal
protection of the Holy Ghost who comes as it were to fill
in the outline of the work of our sanctification by imitation.
Christ lives and works in us in order to transform us into
Himself, but He only works through the Holy Spirit who is
in truth His Spirit. Jesus Christ, we might say, is a divine
symphony, and what his hand is to the musician who performs
it so is the Holy Ghost to the Father, *digitus paternae dexterae*,
finger of God's right hand. Delicately touching the keyboard
of our virtues, with the wonderful power of His gifts, He
brings forth in our souls the heavenly harmony of sanctity,
the sanctity of our Saviour.

He is the *Spirit of Wisdom*, the *Light of our hearts,* who
teaches us to know Christ more fully and more lovingly,
which is the only basis for imitation : the *Fire of Love*, who
enkindles the love for Christ in our souls : the *Spiritual
Unction* who inspires us with desire for our Redeemer and
the wish to resemble Him : the *Spirit of Fortitude* who forges
the stuff of heroes and martyrs out of our souls. The *Sanctifying Spirit*, the Holy Ghost, is the principle and soul of our
work of imitation. Whoever allows himself to be led by
the Holy Ghost becomes at one and the same time the child
of God, His brother and friend, and the imitator of Jesus
Christ.

The creative Spirit, He will renew our entire spiritual life
and illuminate every page of it with the mark of Christ
if only He will come down and dwell in our souls ; He
will not come unless we ask Him. We must call Him by
means of ardent and continual appeal : *Veni, Creator Spiritus!*
Veni, Sancte Spiritus! Veni, Pater pauperum! O come
Thou Father of the poor, who will fill with gifts all who
know how to ask. Each new Pentecost is the result of
perseverance in prayer, as in the Upper Room when " all
these were persevering with one mind in prayer." [1]

It is a regrettable fact that devotion to the Holy Ghost
does not always occupy, we could even go so far as to say it
rarely occupies, the place it deserves in the spiritual life of
Christians, of religious and of priests. This omission is
doubly regrettable if it occurs in the life of one who is trying
to imitate Christ. The imitator of Christ is dedicated to a
profound interior life, of which the Holy Ghost is the supreme
Master, and to the carving out of a pattern of sanctity, of
which the Holy Ghost is the incomparable artist. We have
seen how essential is the help of the Holy Ghost in reproducing
Christ in ourselves and so we need only to reiterate the vital
necessity of asking Him for it. If it is impossible, as Saint
Paul asserts, even to pronounce the name of Jesus without the
Holy Ghost, [2] obviously it is much more impossible to
reproduce Christ in ourselves. The Holy Ghost is the Soul of
the Mystical Body, and He is the soul, the inner and active
principle, we repeat, of our work of imitation. But His
creative activity is conditioned by the strength of our
supplication.

Let us then appeal to the Holy Ghost. After the *Our
Father* and the *Hail Mary,* there is hardly a more ardent prayer
than the *Veni Sancte Spiritus,* the Sequence in the Mass of
Pentecost. It is even more than a prayer, it is a cry of desire
and of love. Many religious Rules prescribe the recitation
of this prayer more or less regularly. We recommend its
recitation apart from inclusion at the beginning of our pious
exercises every day, at the outset of all our intellectual or
apostolic work. We must be on our guard, however,

---

[1] Acts i, 14.
[2] I Cor. xii, 3.

against a very easy temptation, common to all vocal prayer, of reciting with the lips only and not the heart, so that the prayer becomes a mere empty routine. Yet it is easy, too, to put into the little word *Veni* all the vehemence of insatiable desire and irresistible appeal.

Come O Holy Spirit this day into my soul, as once before You descended into the womb of the Blessed Virgin. Cover me in the mighty shadow of Your love, and bring forth the mystical Christ in me, even as You fashioned His corporal body in His Mother's womb. Come and dwell in me until death, that You may continue this divine generation, O most sweet Guest of my soul. Come Holy Ghost, Creator, come, for it is good that you start to work on nothingness.

Sine tuo numine,	If thou take thy grace away,
Nihil est in homine,	Nothing pure in man will stay ;
Nihil est innoxium.	All his good is turned to ill.

Distributor of Your great gifts and Father of the poor, come and bring to me the virtues of Christ and the grace of imitation.

Et emitte coelitus lucis tuae radium . . . The grace of light
Lumen cordium et spiritalis unctio . . . The grace of unction
In labore requies, in aestu temperies, infirma nostris corporis virtute firmans perpeti . . .

The grace of strength

Lava quod est sordidum . . . The grace of purification
Ductore sic te praevio, vitemus omne noxium . . .

The grace above all of charity

Infunde amorem cordibus . . . *ignis* . . . *caritas* . . . *reple tuorum corda fidelium* . . .

The grace of knowing the Father and the Son, and the knowledge of how to follow Christ.

Each one of our calls of *Veni* could bring the Holy Spirit of sevenfold gifts winging to us and hovering above us as He did above Christ on the banks of the Jordan, so that He would communicate again as He did to Christ, His gifts of wisdom, understanding, counsel, fortitude, knowledge, piety and fear of the Lord. What a transformation into

Christ would such daily and continual prayers to the Holy Ghost achieve for us !

Such prayer should become more humble and constant as the time of Pentecost approaches.   Saint Alphonsus considers that a novena is a most important preparation for it, composed of pious exercises and above all of fervent prayers. To this end the Saint composed ten prayers and seven supplications, one for each of the gifts.   We ought to use both, the prayers to awaken in our hearts lively love and desire to imitate Jesus, and the supplications to obtain by the enrichment of the Pentecostal gifts, the delicate sensibility and heroic docility of Christ to the work of grace.   The Upper Room was the first home of the closed retreat, where the work of the spiritual recluses consisted almost entirely in one collective, unanimous and persevering prayer.   The result of such prayer we know.   It was a prodigious and dramatic outpouring of the Holy Spirit, a conflagration which propagated on all sides was intended to embrace the entire world. Obviously Pentecost is the feast of the fire of the apostolate. Twelve poor men, terrified, weak, ignorant, were transformed at one stroke into veritable trumpets of the Truth and martyrs of charity, disciples this time worthy of their Master, and capable of drinking from the same chalice as He did.

It depends on ourselves whether we achieve again and in a small way the miracle of Pentecost.   To do so we need to pray and pray unceasingly. Ask the Blessed Virgin to unite her prayers with ours.   Beg of Christ to send us His Paraclete. Entreat of the Holy Spirit Himself to come, so that He may make of us, poor, sinful and weak, magnificent apostles, true copies of our Divine Redeemer.

CHAPTER 22

THE CULT OF THE BLESSED VIRGIN

IN the mighty work of the Incarnation and of the Redemption our Lady is the collaborator with the Word and with the Holy Ghost. She occupies the same essential rôle in the work of the sanctification of souls. Her ideal and perfect holiness, her double dignity as the Mother of God and the Mother of men, and her function of mediatrix and treasurer of all graces, obtain for her a place of immense importance in our work of imitation of Christ.

Incomparable as she is in her perfection, the very replica of her divine Son, with the sweetest and most human of qualities as befits a woman and a mother, it would be sufficient for us to contemplate and to imitate her in order to reproduce in our souls the image of the Redeemer. She is such an exact copy of our Lord that when we look at her we see Him, and if we try to imitate her and become like her we shall be imitating and resembling Him. *Mirror of Justice*, she reflects Christ without blur or shadow.

Her power to intervene in the generation and development of the Mystical Body of Christ is hers through her office of Mother, her divine and human rôle. She is the Mother of Christ, but she is the Mother of the Whole Christ. She is so filled with Jesus that she overflows with Him and pours Him out into the hearts of all men, and her fruitful, virginal Maternity has expanded through the centuries in spiritual nativities in the souls of all men. Her whole apostolate is the birth and growth of Christ in the Church. In engendering the growth of Jesus in souls she awakens the souls themselves to a spiritual life and intensifies her work as the mother of men whom she thus instructs and nourishes. For any mother, by nature as much as by love, is a born educator. The most holy Virgin, our Mother, takes on then the work of forming and developing our souls and our hearts ; of shaping our wills and our consciences, of turning us into Christians, religious or priests ; in a word, of drawing us up towards a perfect

likeness to our Brother in His ways and in His life. We
are children of the same Mother, who have been educated
by her, and between us, Christ and ourselves, there must
be a family resemblance : like Mother, like Son.

When we proclaim Mary as the treasurer and distributor
of graces, which naturally include the graces of imitating her
divine Son, we are simply confirming the fact that she is
primarily a Mother. She could indeed say with Saint Paul :
" My little children of whom I am in labour again, until
Christ be formed in you."[1]   However, we must also understand that her powerful and efficacious intervention is to a
great extent dependent on the quality of our Marian devotion.
The more we become her devoted children and the more
she demonstrates that she is our generous Mother, the more
she will form Christ in us. The more we ask her, the more
she will fill us with the special graces of imitation.

$$\star \qquad \star \qquad \star \qquad \star \qquad \star \qquad \star \qquad \star$$

The *Hail Mary* almost always follows the *Veni Creator*, a
symbol and further proof, if you like, of the indissoluble
union between the Blessed Virgin and the Holy Ghost in the
work of our sanctification. The Paraclete, asked by our Lady
and sent by her Divine Son, descends upon us and carries out
the work of our "christification." It is apparent, then, that
we must develop our devotion to the Blessed Virgin, that we
must venerate her, and love her and ask her help. All the
graces of imitation can come to us through the heart and
hands of Mary, but we must ask her for them. We must beg
of her explicitly as our powerful and compassionate Mother
to help us in our effort to transform ourselves into Christ.

We can commence in the morning, speaking to her as
also to our Lord in the daily act of consecration, and asking
that through her help this new day may be filled to overflowing with the thought and the love and the imitation of
Christ. At Cîteaux we are told everything begins and
finishes through Mary. This is a perfection of reliance on the
Blessed Virgin which the sons of Saint Alphonsus will be
very happy to share with the sons of Saint Bernard.

---

[1] Gal. iv, 19.

Three times during the recitation of the *Angelus* there is an opportunity of renewing our contemplation on the three great Agents of the Redemption : the Word, the Holy Ghost and the Blessed Virgin. We can recall that imitation is but a prolongation and complement of the mystery of the Incarnation. We can ask Jesus to come to us : we can ask the Holy Ghost to form Him in us and we can ask the Blessed Virgin to lend her maternal co-operation in this new, mystical generation of Christ. During the months before He was born the Blessed Virgin gave to the Word the fulness of His humanity. Let us ask her now that by her example, and by her help, throughout our lives we may cause Christ to grow and expand in ourselves, so that He may become the flower of our souls as He was the flower of her virginal flesh.

Every day, too, we have the opportunity of offering to our Lady the gift of fifty, or one hundred and fifty, *Hail Marys* in our recitation of the Rosary. Let us ensure that the soaring and sinking of the soul from the heights of contemplation to the humble depths of supplication always accompany the mere movement of the lips and of the hands as the beads slip through. The Rosary is always a supplication, and so once again we ask for the realisation in ourselves of the graces, the virtues and the sanctity which belong to her divine Son and herself. We repeat a hundred times : " Holy Mary, Mother of God, pray for us sinners now . . . pray for us . . . help us . . . stretch out your maternal hand and draw us into the light of sinlessness and of love ; raise us up to yourself and through you to Jesus Christ."

We have formed already the habit of meditating during the Rosary on the virtue of the months. We can make this virtue the object of our special prayer at the end of each decade and the beginning of each mystery. A novena is a good way of preparing for the principal feasts of the Blessed Virgin. Let it be a novena of mortification and special, fervent prayers for our greatest need . . . all the efficacious graces of imitation. Consecration to the Blessed Virgin is another Marian practice especially dear to Saint Alphonsus which would be very simple to incorporate into our method of self-sanctification. To consecrate oneself is to alienate oneself from self-love in order to become the property of the Blessed Virgin : to become her child, a child whom henceforth she will protect, educate and shape in her own likeness and thence into the likeness of her Son.

It is a pious custom, too, to recite the *Hail Mary* frequently during the course of the day. It helps us to obtain the grace of practising perfectly the virtue of the month. If we are saying it in our cell, we can say it with our arms outstretched facing the crucifix and a picture of the Blessed Virgin. We can add to it the invocation : " O Jesus, model of charity and of humility, make my heart like unto Thine." It is a simple gesture, to stretch out our arms, but it is very expressive and will serve to remind us straightaway of the ideal of our lives, the imitation of Christ crucified.

With regard to the other prayers to our Lady which recur frequently during the day, such as the Little Office, the litanies, the antiphons, the Office of the Immaculate Conception, we can use all these too from the point of view of imitation. In a word, we can pray all the time to our Lady that we may ourselves be born of her, as the Redeemer was born of her, and that we may come to resemble our elder Brother. All such ardent and continuous prayers to Christ, to the Holy Ghost and to the Blessed Virgin will certainly draw down upon the soul an extraordinary flood of graces. All that remains then is to put these divine energies to the right use in the achievement of our desire to imitate Jesus our Model.

CHAPTER 23

ACTION AND REACTION

THE two great laws which direct our method of self-sanctification, namely contemplation and prayer, call into being a third one, the law of activity. We do not contemplate for the mere sake of contemplation, but in order to reproduce in ourselves the object of our thought. We do not pray purely for the sake of praying, but in order to obtain the grace to act. Prayer is productive of grace, and grace in its turn is the principle of action. Therefore contemplation and prayer are not an end in themselves but simply a means to the action of imitation. Though the reproduction of Christ in ourselves is primarily the work of God, yet of necessity it also requires the labour of man. Saint Paul sums up perfectly the action of imitation when he says : " Yet not I, but the grace of God with me."[1]

We shall set down a definition for this third law too, as for the two preceding, so that we can examine and develop it. It is this :

" The perfect imitation of Jesus Christ consists essentially in a twofold activity. *Reaction* : which is the whole-hearted struggle against all that opposes our perfect resemblance to Christ. *Action* : the practice of the example of the Master, and of all the virtues, with special emphasis on the virtue of the month."

Reaction : This is a comparatively negative activity, in as much as it involves the setting aside or relinquishing of anything which could compromise, diminish or destroy our likeness to Jesus Christ. *Action* : on the other hand is positive work, for it aims at developing and bringing out in the soul all characteristics which bear a resemblance to Christ.

Before we can build anything we must clear away the rubble and the first effort imposed on us in the action of imitation is the successful removal of all obstacles to the reproduction of Jesus Christ ; in particular, sin, our passions,

[1] I Cor. xv, 10.

our faults, and especially certain faults. The sanctity of Christ, which is our ideal, is the fruit of absolute purity of soul. Jesus is innocence itself. There is not the slightest stain or blemish on His soul, which possessed the privilege not only of sinlessness but of impeccability. " Which of you shall convince me of sin ?"[2] He asked His enemies and none dared to challenge Him. This incorruptibility of conscience which is one of the fundamental qualities of our Lord, ought also to be at the base of our imitation of Him. Before acting like our Lord, we must first of all be like Him. Each soul is like a blank canvas on which, unless it is spotless. it would be impossible to reproduce a masterpiece. The principal object of the imitator of Jesus Christ is then to arrive progressively at delicacy of conscience and immunity from sin. Purity of conscience ; absence of mortal sin ; flight from all deliberate venial sin ; slow but continual diminution of all our weakness and imperfection : this is a programme of purification to be realised by daily struggle, by the spirit of penance and by the practice of frequent Confession.

This is a work of reformation and total purification which must be commenced at the source of all evil, namely our own nature weakened by original sin. We must put off the " old man who is corrupted according to the desire of error" before we can put on the " new man, who according to God is created in justice and holiness of truth."[3] Before the new man can rise again with Jesus Christ the old man must first be crucified with Jesus Christ. A farmer cannot sow his seed unless the field has been properly tilled and all noxious weeds removed. Jesus Christ, who is the Seed of God, cannot grow and flourish in our souls unless they too have become like virgin soil. Here in the work of purification of our souls is the role of that interior and exterior mortification which is so constantly recommended by all the masters of the spiritual life. Here is the programme of reaction, the essential condition of imitation which our Lord Himself laid down in the Gospel in that unequivocal statement : "If any man will come after me, let him deny himself, and take up his cross, and follow me."[4]

---

[2] John viii, 46.
[3] Eph. iv, 22–24.   [4] Matt. xvi, 24.

This is *reaction*. It is the fight against all that could form a hindrance or a shadow in our resemblance to Christ ; it is a struggle which finally puts us into a state of purity, harmony, recollection, of submission and preparation, so that we can now take our next step which is *action*.

Now we endeavour to follow the example of our Lord : we try to imitate the interior state of His soul in our souls : we relive His life, either His hidden life of solitude or His apostolate, according to our own circumstances and the inner workings of the Holy Ghost, all within the compass of the will of God as expressed in our Holy Rule, and by our Superiors. What particularly characterises our programme of active imitation, however, is our specific attention to the virtues of Christ, and especially as we follow them in the twelve virtues of the months. Our spiritual activity should be in its general tendency oriented and concentrated towards the acquisition and development in ourselves of the virtues of the Redeemer.

It is particularly fitting that the third " law of imitation " should be one of activity, for the very word virtue implies activity. All virtue is in effect the sum of rightly directed action. Outside the sacraments, which are our sources of divine life, our actions are the generators of progressive virtue. Imitation of Christ consists above all in acting like Jesus Christ, and in practising virtue like Him, fully, continuously, and perseveringly.

Since we wish our imitation to be perfect it follows that our whole lives must be a perfect exercise of the virtues. For there are ways and ways of acting virtuously. In our austere task there can be no hint of nonchalance, of idleness, of drawing to a halt. We must avoid at all costs any half-hearted effort, which could only produce a mere shadow of virtue and nothing but an outline of Jesus our Model. A perfect imitator of Jesus Christ is a perfect practitioner of the virtues, who works hard at them all the time. The whole value of a virtue, according to Saint Thomas, is the intensity, the frequency and the perseverance with which it is practised. Let us examine these qualities. *Intensity* : By this we mean that our acts of virtue must be vigorous and firm. They must be lighted by faith and sustained by all the energies of the will and the enthusiasm of the heart. We must perform them at a high supernatural level with all the joy and rapture of the soul. *Frequency* : Here we require that our entire lives must be purely an effort without break, all thoughts, desires and affections, all words, actions and sufferings, to follow the example of Christ and to achieve a masterpiece of virtue. We mean too that we must be constantly on our guard against allowing empty periods to crop up, when we relax our vigour or stray from our objective. In other words we must produce from the soil, every moment, a full ear of wheat. *Perseverance* : Generosity and immutability are called for here. To persevere we must go forward all the time, never glancing back at the furrow we have ploughed, never once in forty, fifty, sixty years, but, tensed for the effort, we must bend all the energies of our being towards the accomplishment of our task, austere but fruitful, the imitation of Christ. He alone realised the fulness of supernatural action required for the perfect practice of the virtues. It is an intense and permanent activity, and the supreme law of our method of imitation of Christ.

CHAPTER 24

PROGRAMME OF LIFE

THE imitation of Christ is essentially a personal act, promoted by a loving contemplation of the Ideal, and sustained by the source of all grace, prayer. The imitator of the Redeemer lives as He lived, acts and suffers as He acted and suffered, practises virtue as He Himself practised it. According to the method we have proposed the work of reproducing Christ is characterised by its universality and its detail. We must imitate Christ in general, His many aspects, perfections, examples, and we must select just one of His virtues and practise it every month.

A general imitation of Christ would indeed, if wisely carried out, ensure our sanctification. To achieve it we have to transform all the acts of our lives, even the most insignificant or commonplace, into acts of imitation. This is the sublime art of doing the divine work in everything, always, and everywhere as Jesus Christ Himself did ; an art whose tremendous depths and far-reaching results are equalled only by its complete simplicity.

We must remember, however, that while the life of Christ is wonderful in all its aspects, not every one of these is imitable, and those which are cannot necessarily be imitated with equal exactitude. In the life of Jesus, put before us for our faithful imitation, we must consider His divine strength at work in interior acts and exterior works, the eternal Source from whence He came, and the supreme end towards which He was orientated.

The life of our Saviour, like all human life, was made up of an enormous mass of varying actions, occupations, events, and diverse situations. There was His public social life : Jesus Christ was born in a stable at Bethlehem, He was presented at the Temple, fled into Egypt and lived at Nazareth, working as a carpenter, praying, obeying His parents. He went out into the desert, was baptised, commenced His apostolate ; He preached, healed the sick, forgave sinners, consoled the sorrowful, sowed miracles and reaped hatred ; He was betrayed, sold to His enemies, condemned to death and crucified. He died, rose from the dead, ascended into heaven. That is the historical life of the Man-God.

But underlying all this exterior life, as hidden as the water which lurks beneath the green turf in the bog, there was another life, hidden, mysterious, close to God, of which the outer appearance was but the palest reflection : the interior life of Jesus Christ, wholly spiritual and hidden. So it is that we find the most sublime aspects of our Lord not in His works, but in His soul : in His thoughts, in His feelings, in His wishes, and in His powers of contemplation, adoration, praise, abandonment and love.

According to how circumstances permit it we may imitate the exterior life of our Lord within the scope of the Rule and of the various duties of our state. We may follow His examples of generosity, sweetness and patience, of humility and prayer, of mortification and poverty, of hard work and apostolic zeal. The important thing is to imitate Christ not so much in His exterior way but in the things of the spirit ; the great imitation is the imitation of His interior life.

Whatever our state in life may be, or whatever our function or occupation, whether ordinary Christian, religious, priest or mother of a family, professor or missionary ; whether in the church or at the office, in the workshop or at leisure, at work or at prayer, it is always possible to reproduce in ourselves the soul of our Saviour, that is to say His divine dispositions and states of holiness. To follow in our outward lives the footsteps of Christ is often quite impossible, but we are always able to make our own His thoughts and His affections.

Reproductions of great paintings, of Raphael's for example, are often very beautiful in their fidelity to the artist's perspective, his exactitude of design or composition and the purity of his line, but the tonality of his colours and the variety and delicacy of his tints can never be enjoyed but in the original. So with the living reproductions of the life of Jesus Christ, what matters is the design, not the colour ; the design is His interior life, the colour is supplied by His own exterior circumstances.

Now the reproduction in our own souls of the soul of
Jesus Christ has already been found to be most effectively
achieved by loyal attention to the first rule of our system
of imitation, namely, loving, continual and imitative contemplation of Jesus our Model. We have shown also that
prayer, holy Mass, Communion, the Office, the Way of the
Cross, and a variety of exercises in recollection are all in fact
interior imitation of the interior life of our Lord. There
is no need to insist further on it. Besides, the originality
of our general method of imitation depends less on either
the exterior or interior life of Jesus Christ than on the very
principle from which His life emanates, which is the Will
of God.

The primary disposition of the soul of our Lord was loving,
transcendental submission to the will of the Father. His
whole journey through this world, from the instant of the
Incarnation until His last breath on Calvary was designed
within the immutable framework of the Divine Will. He
did literally nothing which was not inspired and motivated
by obedience. In fact, the whole life of the Redeemer
is one glorious *Fiat* of adoration and love. " My meat is
to do the will of him that sent me."[1]

Before the horrors of His Passion and in the depths
of His agony the same cry from the heart passes His lips :
" not as I will, but as thou wilt."[2] Such adherence to the
will of God was the soul of His own prayer, the *Pater Noster*,
and the work of His whole life. In the successive stages and
the different situations of His earthly sojourn, no matter
what were the thousand and one different activities in which
He was engaged He was really doing only one thing : the
will of the Father.

Obviously here is the guiding light for us. Our general
imitation of Jesus our Model should consist simply in reproducing in ourselves that which is deepest and holiest in Him :
namely His submission to God. Following His example
we want to shape our lives on the solid foundation and within
the unalterable compass of the will of God and its accomplishment. Like our Saviour we want never to act in any way

[1] John iv, 34.
[2] Matt. xxvi, 39.

against or outside of this Divine Will, and like Him also we
wish to do and to suffer all things in conformity with it. It
matters not at all whether we are here or there, doing this
action or that. The essential, the *unum necessarium*, is to be
where the Father wishes us to be, to be doing what He wills.
Everything else is accidental, pointless, possibly dangerous,
maybe even wrong. As our Lord was able to say at every ·
moment: "I do always the things that please Him,"[3] so we
too should be in the position at all times to say : " I imitate
Jesus Christ."

We can go a long way towards achieving this by
accustoming ourselves with deliberate obstinacy to dwell only
within the confines of the Divine Will as expressed in the
Ten Commandments and the Precepts of the Church, the
holy Rule, our Superiors, the duties of our state of life, the
dispositions of Providence, and the inspirations of the
Holy Ghost. Thus to desire the will of God and to make our
actions the consequence of this desire, is to imitate Jesus Christ
in the most complete and sublime way. We can consolidate
this state of mind and soul from time to time, in accordance
with the strength of our spiritual life and the calls of grace,
by renewing, before every action, a fervent resolution to
accomplish, like Jesus, the will of God.

Fiat voluntas tua ! There is another aspect, however, of
this basis for our imitation of Christ. We want to achieve
the Divine Will with the *same intention* as Jesus Christ. " For
let this mind be in you, which was also in Christ Jesus."[4]
It is a philosophic and moral truth that the end specifies
the act. We might extend that and say that the end specifies
the life. The quality of a life, its frivolity or nobility, its
impiety or holiness, depends in large part on its orientation,
on the purpose which it is serving. What matters is not so
much what one does as the manner in which and the motive
for which one does it. A man who is a hero in our human eyes
may in God's sight be a most wretched sinner. A life which
outwardly appears splendid in reality may be infamous,
if a man's soul is base and his intentions worthless. At the
day of judgment there will certainly be many celebrities

---

[3] John viii, 29.
[4] Phil ii, 5.

tumbling from their pedestals ! Washing dishes, sweeping a corridor, picking up a wisp of straw are all divine and immortal works if they are included in the scope of the right intention.

The life of Christ is good both in itself and in its purpose. The Incarnation, the Passion, the Redemption, the Holy Eucharist, the Church, are all directed to the glory of God and the salvation of the world, for Christ could not but have the glory of God, which is the supreme end of all the order of creation both natural and supernatural constantly before Him. In His thirty-three years there is nothing which was not a ray of glory for the Holy Trinity, or an instrument of universal salvation. "I seek not my own glory"; "My glory is nothing."[5] The basis of His own prayer was the glory of God, and at the eve of His death, looking back over His life on earth He was able to say that He had indeed accomplished His task and glorified God. "I have glorified thee on earth; I have finished the work which thou gavest me to do."[6] His task was the Redemption. For this He became man, worked, suffered, died and rose again. "For the Son of man is come to save that which was lost."[7] "I am come that they may have life and may have it more abundantly."[8] The conquest of souls for the glory of the Father was the sum of His life.

The glory of God and the salvation of the world is the supreme and ultimate answer to the "Why?" of our lives too. What is there for the Christian, the religious, the priest, to desire or to search for except that which Jesus Christ has already desired and sought ? In other words, the imitator of Jesus our Model will always, as He did, perform the will of the Father, and perform it always with the same intentions : God and souls. This concern for the glory of God was a passion with all the saints. We are familiar with the *ad majorem Dei gloriam* of Saint Ignatius. Of Saint Alphonsus it was said : "Bishop Liguori has nothing in his head but the glory of God !" "Do all for the glory of God," says Saint Paul.[9]

[5] John viii, 50, 54.
[6] *Id.* xvii, 4.
[7] Matt. xviii, 11.
[8] John x, 10.
[9] I Cor. x, 31.

We could multiply instances of this saintly obsession. Following the example of our Lord, who, eating, drinking, resting or sleeping, glorified the Father infinitely and redeemed humanity, we must in all our acts, however insignificant, and in our lowliest labours guard the purity and sublimity of our intention. We work, pray, do all and suffer all exclusively for God and the apostolate. Yet since this good intention has always the tendency to deviate and to weaken, we must renew it often, at each hour of the day and at the start of each new occupation.

Precise, definite and continuous imitation of Jesus Christ is no longer then a dream but a reality. To anyone who asks us " What are you doing ? " we can now answer without hesitation : " I am imitating Jesus Christ. Like Him, now and all the time I am doing the Divine Will for the glory of the Father and the salvation of souls." Thus our existences, too often narrow, prosy and flat, will be utterly transformed ; immense horizons and a heroic destiny open up before them, as they become enlarged, uplifted, sanctified. There will be no more meanness, or ugliness, no more evil in the life that has been exalted by the purity of its intention to the level of Christ.

This general process of imitation besides including the exercise of perfect charity has the further advantage of implying the reaction, indirect without doubt, but powerful and continual against all in us which might work against the reproduction of Jesus Christ : reaction against mortal and venial sin, against voluntary imperfections and resistance to grace, and against the weaknesses and passions which are their cause. No one can constantly and generously practise the most perfect conformity to the Divine Will, keep the commandments of God and of the Church, become the voluntary slave of the Rule, of Superiors and the duties of his state, without acquiring a virginal purity of conscience and progressively triumphing over his evil tendencies. The exclusive and magnificent pursuit of the glory of God and the salvation of souls is a panacea for all spiritual ills, mean little vanities, self-esteem and childish susceptibilities of pride. It is God who has entered and conquered the soul, driving out the great enemy of Jesus Christ, egoism.

Let us recapitulate and define :

1. We must maintain the strong and immovable disposition, like Jesus Christ, to accomplish always and everywhere the will of God.

2. In all our prayers we must make the general resolution to follow the example of our Redeemer and perform throughout the course of every day the will of God, for the glory of the Father and the salvation of souls.

3. Before each action, at every quarter of an hour if possible, we should renew briefly, but with great fervour, this good intention : My God, like Jesus Christ I wish to do Your will for Your glory and the good of souls.

CHAPTER 25

THE VIRTUES OF THE MONTH

IMITATION of Christ is the reproduction of Christ in general and in particular. In general we imitate His whole life ; in detail we select for our model this or that one of His virtues. Hence the necessity to speak more fully of the process of imitating Him in detail, as we have just done of the general process.

Each month we shall choose one of Christ's virtues and endeavour to follow His example in our way of practising it. This comparatively restricted imitation depends for its success on the quality of our actions and the number of times we perform them. Obviously the more we act in a virtuous manner the more we shall grow to resemble our Ideal, and the manner of ensuring the success of our labour of love is to choose excellent resolutions and to persevere in the keeping of them.

What exactly do we mean by resolution ? We mean not a desire, or a whim or fancy, but a strong unwavering decision of the will, which knows what it chooses and which deliberately assents. However, we must take care not to confuse resolution with *resolutions*. Resolution is one and invariable, a quality which is identical in all who possess it ; it aspires to an ideal, which in our case is perfect resemblance to Jesus our Model ; and it takes the practical form of which we have just spoken, general imitation of Christ. It is the resolution to imitate Jesus Christ perfectly through the universal accomplishment of the Divine Will for the glory of the Father and the redemption of souls. Do we fully recognise the profound influence on the spiritual life of such resolution ? One would like to believe so. The doctors of the Church in all cases, and the saints, insist on its primordial and basic rôle, for it is the fulness of that goodwill without which nothing is achieved or could be achieved. When Saint Thomas was asked by a religious sister on an occasion what one required to become a saint, he replied laconically :

" The will." But let us pass for the moment to particular *resolutions*.

Resolution is, as it were, the trunk from which spring the shoots of the particular resolutions. On the worth of these and our faithfulness in keeping them depends the effect of the virtue and indeed of the imitation itself of Jesus Christ. Making and keeping them is a delicate art which can be resolved into two axioms : know what to choose, and know how to practise what you choose. Vigour, precision, discretion, earnestness and simplicity : such are the qualities which will sustain our monthly programme.

To begin with vigour : this particular resolution, just like the general resolution, is a full act of the will. It is a decision hewn not in clay but in granite or marble. It is something which must be kept, and which if so kept will cling to the soul like a mighty oak to the soil, so that shaken, buffeted, wracked, it will still stand.

To vigour let us add precision : let us in fact avoid at all costs vagueness or nebulous ideas. What distinguishes the particular resolution from the general one is precisely the clarity of its object. We must have precision in regard to an interior or exterior act, in practising or avoiding an action. For instance, we decide that no word of criticism shall cross our lips : an exterior act which we have resolved to *avoid*. We must be precise regarding the number of times we perform an action : let us say, twenty *acts* of humility every day. We must be definite as to the times we practise a certain virtue : for instance, let us place ourselves in the presence of God every quarter of an hour, or before each new occupation. The more precise our resolutions are the better they will be, because we can control them. Some people write them down, which is quite an excellent habit since it precludes any lapses of memory.

Let us also introduce discretion into our choice of resolutions. for there is no point in multiplying them to excess. Anyone starting two hares at one time catches neither. So, instead of wasting our energies let us rather concentrate them, for spiritual quixoticism will not purchase the luxury of a heroic programme. Beware of illusions, children of presumption and begetters of discouragement ! We must have a sense of proportion, and keep equally far from the insignificant or the sublime. Desiring neither too much nor too little, let us be content with a serious and commonsense programme. The sensible and practical resolution is one which taking count of all moral potentialities, such as temperament, character, acquired virtue, faults, the inspirations of grace, prompts generous efforts of practical possibilities.

There are, of course, two kinds of efforts to be made, one negative and the other positive. It will sometimes be necessary, especially at the outset of the spiritual life, to act *negatively*, that is, for example, to subdue a passion, to get rid of a habit, to fill in a gap, any of which may be influencing the soul in the direct opposite of the virtue of the month. For instance, we may have to form the resolution *not* to be impatient or fretful, *not* to criticise authority, or *not* to fritter away the time for prayer. Alternatively we must of course aim by both interior and exterior action *positively* to develop the virtue, strengthening its different aspects, whether essential or secondary : for instance, the resolution to pray with more faith or humility ; to cultivate the habit of seeing God in our Superiors in a greater or fuller degree, and our Lord among our brethren, in order the more perfectly to imitate His charity and His obedience.

Once again we would stress the importance of simplicity. Simplicity is the very gauge of success, just as truly as complexity is the cause of failure. Modern life overcharged as it is with pointless activity lends itself more easily to all sorts of entanglements. Let us tend to simplify our approach all the time, without losing anything of importance to our success. We can do this in two ways : first of all by integrating our resolutions with our Rule, or our rule of life, and the scope of our daily occupations : secondly by perfecting our activities rather than adding to them, because true progress is much more a matter of quality than of mere quantity. Instead of multiplying a lot of weak or shallow acts of virtue, it is far more important to intensify some and to endow them with supernatural strength and moral vigour. In other words it is greatly preferable to fortify the position we have conquered than to try to take new ones.

Similarly with regard to prayer and supplication, the

tendency to simplify should always prevail. When we have completed our meditation and concluded our examination of conscience we may try to demonstrate our faithful adherence to all the pious exercises of custom, tradition and even supererogation. But of what use are these if they are vitiated by routine, by distraction, by sluggishness? What is to be gained by overloading ourselves with extra practices and thereby adding mediocrity to mediocrity? It is good here to recall our Lord's counsel : " And when you are praying, speak not much, as the heathens. For they think that in their much speaking they may be heard."[1]

One cry from the heart is far more powerful than a hundred words from the lips. We pray enough : let us pray better. To achieve that we shall perfect all our pious exercises by preceding them with a perfect act of faith in the presence of God, and of humility and trust in Him.

Another point, which is a commonplace in asceticism, is the unending struggle against the dominant passion or fault. Any form of spirituality which overlooked or disdained this dour and difficult side of life of the spirit ought to be viewed with the utmost caution, and suspected of developing into the illusion of semi-quietism. The words of Christ remain for us all to see . . . " If any man will come after me . . . " Before following the Master, therefore, it is necessary to deny ourselves ; and that is self-abnegation, the basis of our imitation.

Our method of sanctification, while putting the accent on the " Follow me " cannot and should not omit the " Deny yourself." This can be condensed into the formula of the third law of our method of imitation, namely action and reaction. There must be reaction against all that gets in the way of our perfect reproduction of Jesus Christ, particularly strong and vigorous against our predominant fault or passion. This reaction can in its turn find a point of contact with a secondary resolution which in order to guard us from a scattering of our efforts could harmonise easily with the virtue of the month, thus killing two birds with one stone.

For example : Dominant Passion, Pride.

January : *Virtue of the Month* : *Faith.*

We shall be making frequent acts of faith, so let us make

---
[1] Matt. vi, 7.

them in the words of Christ which remind us of humility :
" Blessed are the meek for they shall possess the land."[2]
Or again : " Unless you become as little children, you shall
not enter into the kingdom of heaven."[3] " Every one that
exalteth himself, shall be humbled ; and he that humbleth
himself, shall be exalted."[4]

February : Virtue of the Month : Hope.

We shall repeat continuously, as our ejaculatory prayer :
I am nothing, but " I can do all things in Him who strength-
eneth me."[5] Such confidence in God is at once a lack of trust
in ourselves and a recognition of our own pettiness.

July : Virtue of the Month : Obedience.

We shall here make the resolution to re-emphasise by our
own humility our respect for authority, and not to criticise
or pronounce judgement on it.

Finally, it would be an excellent thing during the course
of the day to go over and remake these particular resolutions,
at the end of each period of prayer and at the two examinations
at midday and in the evening.

Having decided upon the course to follow, all that remains
now is to adhere to it with generosity, loyalty and perseverance. We must not draw back before its difficulty and
before the sacrifice inherent in the exercise of any virtue,
especially the passive virtues such as obedience, humility,
detachment and self-abnegation. We must mobilise all
our forces for action, and avoid all abortive efforts since
only mature and prepared action can lay the foundation for
any habit. The perfection of a virtue can only come through
perfecting acts of this virtue. Let us always strive for lofti-
ness of soul, for nobility is not to be found in the intrinsic
grandeur but in the purpose of an act. The sublime motive
can often mix with the ordinary, even trivial, action. The
important thing is to know how to stand by our resolutions,
so that we may arrive at the smooth and habitual practice of
some pre-eminent virtue. We need to practise these resolutions with earnestness and fidelity, for they are not just a

---

[2] Matt. v, 4.
[3] *Id.* xviii, 3.
[4] Luke xiv, 11.
[5] Phil. iv, 13.

suggested ideal, approached with a long-term outlook, but a challenging programme of life here and now realisable. Obviously we must practise them carefully and all the time. It is possible that we may hesitate over making them, but once we have embarked on them, any voluntary withdrawal would be weakness and failure. If we do fail in any of them, through forgetfulness, distraction or idleness, we must recover at once, ask pardon of God, impose a penance upon ourselves, and firmly strengthen our flagging wills. Such work will continue throughout the month without cessation or discouragement, and will be accompanied and sustained by continual prayer and supplication to Jesus and Mary.

Finally and above all we must be on the watch to see that we are acting virtuously and faithfully following our programme of imitation only with the same outlook of Jesus Christ and the desire to reproduce Him exactly. We do not cultivate the virtues for their own sakes, but for love of Him, for the same motives and with the same sentiments that animated Him, that is to say, the glory of God and the salvation of the world.

SUMMARY

1. Preparation at the beginning of the month : make in writing certain definite and practical resolutions, few in number.

2. During the course of the day endeavour at fixed times to keep them faithfully and perfectly, in imitation of Jesus Christ, for the glory of God and the redemption of souls.

3. Remake these resolutions firmly at all times of prayer, and each examination of conscience.

CHAPTER 26

EXAMINATION AND CONFESSION

THE twin approach, particular and general, to imitation of Christ, of which we have just been speaking, if it is to succeed completely will need to be regularly and carefully revised. That revision leads us to the fourth law of our system. Though perhaps not as important as the other three, yet it must not be regarded as superfluous, or as unnecessarily confining or pedantic. As in the case of the others we shall give our definition of it, and specify its precise application.

The perfect imitation of Jesus Christ requires as a complementary factor perfect control of that imitation.

The spiritual writers and the saints are all in agreement in advising and imposing this control, which has become one of universal practice. Saint Benedict requires in the Rule that ' each soul shall at all times watch over all the acts of his life.' Saint Teresa advises : " In each of your actions and at every hour of the day, examine your conscience, and after reviewing your faults, endeavour to correct them with the help of God. By this means you will attain perfection." Saint Catherine of Siena based her entire spiritual doctrine on a twofold knowledge : of God and of oneself ; the first is the fruit of prayer and the second, the result of profound and detailed study of one's being and one's way of life. Among all the Orders and Congregations there is not one which has not inscribed in its programme for spiritual progress and the interior life, examination of conscience, both particular and general.

Carefully exercised, such moral control is at all times illuminating to the spirit, salutary for the conscience and stimulating to the will. It is a light which reveals our weakness and promotes humility and confidence in God ; it is a constructive force which moves us to repentance in the face of our failings and it is a spur which urges us on to the right road again. To obtain a frank and reliable evaluation

of what we are and what we are worth we need both frequent examination of the soul and firm control of our way
of life. Many illusions are born of a flight from self and a
reluctance to assess oneself, and many spiritual failings derive
from a failure to keep check.

Our ascetic programme is crystallised around our Lord
in the form of imitation of Him, and nothing can therefore
be more logical than that such imitation should be subjected
to a general law of control. It is necessary, too, that the
control to be fully effective should be precise as well as general.
That is why it is opportune to add to the obligatory particular
examination other optional examinations of a more general
nature. To the daily account add the weekly and the annual
balance sheet. In principle, and in fact, this control ought
to be regularly and minutely exercised within the scheme
of our imitation and within the scope of our method of
contemplation, prayer and activity.

We now come to the practical way of organising this
inspection. For everyone attempting a genuine, progressive and constant imitation of Christ, we suggest the following
four occasions for appraising one's efforts : a particular
examination at midday, a general examination in the evening,
weekly examination when going to Confession, and an
annual examination on the occasion of the retreat.

The majority of Rules and Constitutions prescribe the
particular examination ; obligatory for religious members
of the Orders, it is also strongly recommended for all priests
and laity endeavouring to lead the spiritual life. No one
will be surprised to learn that of all pious exercises this
examination is the one most easily omitted or most negligently
fulfilled. Could this be because it is also the most productive
of good results ? If fidelity to this daily check is an acquired
virtue, and one which is common to all spiritual people,
obviously the perfection of such a virtue must have far-
reaching effects. In order to remedy one's many deficiencies
it would be useful to conceive of and to practice it under
the form of a spiritual confession in the same way as we
make a spiritual communion.

Confession is the sacrament which retrieves all our best
interior dispositions : confession of sin, contrition, firm

purpose of amendment, and a penance. In the privacy of our conscience we make our confession direct to Jesus Christ, and nothing could be more simple, or more moving and vital, or less subject to distraction. It is an act of faith in the presence of Christ, actually in the tabernacle, mystically in the sanctuary of our souls. Like Mary Magdalen we kneel humbly in spirit at His feet, and glance quickly at the way in which we are holding to our particular resolutions. If we are being true, let us give thanks to Him, but if we are wavering, then we shall admit our failures and omissions with truth, and follow this at once with an act of contrition. " Jesus I love You, but I love You so little, and so badly . . . forgive me. I promised You to walk in Your footsteps, to be, like You, gentle and patient, charitable and silent . . . But unfortunately I have broken my word and offended Your loving Heart . . . Adored Master, pardon me . . . in expiation of my lukewarmness I will impose on myself . . . (name a penance). But I am coming again to You . . . resolved to do better. I offer You my resolutions in testimony of my love. Once again I promise You to imitate You . . . and to resemble You in (name a resolution). O Jesus, whatever happens, even to death itself, I will remain faithful to You. Faithful . . . so long as You, O Lord, will help me. You know my weakness . . . my inconstancy. Give me all Your graces : strength and generosity and perseverance. With You I can do all things . . . without You, nothing."

" O Mary, the former of Christ in me, help me to keep all my resolutions to-day."

After a particular examination such as this we must certainly be restored to Christ, pardoned, purified and comforted, and disposed more than ever to continue the great work of imitation with all our strength and wills.

The particular examination at midday will be extended and complemented by the general examination in the evening. We may add to it also a quick check on our practice of the virtue of the month. What must characterise this inquiry, however, and distinguish it from the former is the scope of its object, which is the general process of imitation.

Let us pose the two following questions and answer them truthfully :

First : How far have we today followed Christ's example
by faithful conformity with the will of God ? That is to
say, have we kept the commandments of God and of the
Church and avoided all sin ? Have we meticulously kept
the Rule ? Have we nothing to reproach ourselves with
in respect of obedience to Superiors ? Have the duties of
our state, priest, missionary, educator, been accomplished
with exactitude ? How docilely have we responded to the
inspirations of grace ?

Second : In following Christ's example in the accomplishment of the Divine Will have we consistently sought, without self-satisfaction, the glory of God and the salvation of
the world ? Have we dwelt on the purity and depth of this
intention, renewing it often during the course of the day ?

Let us make a spiritual confession to Jesus out of this
examination also, and end it, like the particular examination,
with repentance, a renewal of the general resolution and a
prayer. Thus practised, such control fits in very suitably
with our method of imitation of Christ and also constitutes
an excellent remote preparation for the Sacrament of Penance.

Confession plays too important a role in the spiritual
life to be passed over in silence. To speak of it at this point
implies that we are going to review our whole work of
imitation. Confession emphasises the resemblance between
the soul and Christ, for in thus examining our sins we can
make our own the thoughts and reactions, and the attitude
of our Lord when face to face with sin. Like Jesus Christ
we can then see sin for what it is, the mystery of iniquity, the
destruction of the glory of God, the assassin of souls, and with
Jesus Christ we can feel the horror of and the hatred for its
malignity. Following His example we can fight it, and be
ready to suffer, even to die, in order to annihilate it in ourselves and around us, and to raise on its ruins the kingdom
of God. For this is the whole work of the apostolate. These
are the conditions of soul necessary for confession in the true
imitator of Jesus our Model. We must have a completely
pure conscience on to which can be projected the holiness
of Jesus Christ. The sacrament of purification, Confession,
has a two-fold force of cleaning and preserving. It is a
second baptism effacing all spiritual ills and clearing away

all mists and shadows from the heart.   There is no stain
which can resist the Blood of Christ and the sorrow of the
penitent.   Then, and this is an aspect of Penance which is
too often overlooked, having cleaned away the past it immun-
ises, as it were, the future, granting special graces of prudence
and of strength to help us to avoid the mud and the pitfalls,
and to draw us little by little closer to the immaculate holiness
of Jesus our Model.   At the same time, however, it is obvious
that the sacrament is a source of purity only in proportion
to the dispositions of purity with which it is received.   Hence
the need for a careful and perfect preparation.   Here again
as in all the previous pious exercises touched upon, the imitator
of Christ has his own original method of confession, which
is within the scope of the work of imitation.   His art consists
in transforming the disagreeable drudgery which unfortunately it so often is, into an act of friendship with Jesus
Christ.   Each of his confessions, then, becomes a confession
of love ;   in other words it is a confession inspired by love,
and of which all the elements, examination of conscience,
contrition and firm purpose of amendment are impregnated
with charity.

The examination reveals the conscience in the light of love,
for not only intelligence and memory enter upon this work
but also the heart, the source of love.   It will not be merely
an examination either which just recapitulates the particular
and general examinations of the past week.   Because of our
friendship with Jesus our Model we shall go over our daily
lives searching for any point of difference from His, for anything, however slight, which was in opposition to the will of
God and outside of our dedication to the glory of God and
the salvation of souls.   We shall find many imperfections by
the light of this love !   True love is penetrating and inexorable
and when turned upon the conscience it discerns immediately
the slightest grain of dust or the lightest cloud of mist.   Just
as a ray of sunlight piercing a blind reveals millions of tiny
atoms in the air, so the divine love falling upon the soul
discloses its many thousands of imperfections.   Otherwise why
should the saints have always been accusing themselves
of faults and worthlessness, but that they loved so much that
they were able to see their interior lives with startling clarity.

After accompanying and helping the examination of conscience, the love of Christ will promote and sanctify the contrition. Contrition is one of the most powerful and purifying forms of love. The author of *The Imitation* urges us to "burn and consume all our sins in the fire of divine charity."[1] We shall endeavour, then, to regret all our betrayals of Jesus Christ, through pure love, to console Him and please Him, and to draw nearer to Him ourselves. Let this sorrow be very deep. Be sure that it comes from the very depths of the soul by contemplating our Lord upon the Cross and sustaining the feeling of remorse through the sight of His open wounds and grief-stricken heart.

Confession will find its complete perfection and fulfilment in the efficacy of the firm purpose of amendment, built upon love. One of the main causes of spiritual mediocrity and the partial sterility of so many confessions is the inconstancy with which this purpose is kept. If the purifying power of the sacrament depends upon the intensity of contrition, its preservative force rests upon the quality of the firm purpose of amendment. But if this in its turn is to be an unyielding barrier against evil it must hinge upon love. We do not know how to form a purpose at all unless we love.

That great psychologist, Saint Alphonsus said to his missionaries : "Preach the love of Jesus Christ. None of the conversions which are based upon the fear of hell alone endure. Fear passes, and people fall again into sin. But when anyone is converted from sin through the love of Jesus Christ, then he will certainly persevere." Confession, then, is essentially a conversion, since to be converted is to be turned back and placed again on the right road. We are not always on the right road, nor going in the direction we should, and so we shall base our firm purpose of amendment on the friendship of Christ and say to Him : " O, Lord, for the future no more sin, no further resistance to grace, or manifestations of pride or sensuality . . . and for the reason that I love You, and I wish to resemble You more and more in purity of conscience. I wish to be like You because I love You with all my heart and all my soul and all my strength." For the imitative love of Christ is as essential to the firm purpose of

---

[1] *Imit.* Bk. 4, ch. 9.

amendment as was the flying buttress to the Gothic cathedral. Without the love of Jesus Christ our good intentions would yield like a crumbling wall at the first push.

With regard to the penance given to us, let us form the habit of doing it at once, before the crucifix and in union with Jesus, the Victim of expiation for all the sins of the world . . . . including our own.

All these actions relative to Confession should be accompanied by prayer. Penitence is a virtue which is excellent to practise, but it is essential that we ask for it first. Like the leper in the Gospel, let us throw ourselves at the feet of Jesus and cry : " Lord, if thou wilt, thou canst make me clean." And Jesus will reply : " I will. Be thou cleansed." [2]

Such should be the confession of the religious, the imitator of Jesus Christ. A purifying of the soul in love, where we regain some little part of our baptismal innocence and participate a little more intimately in the spotlessness of Christ, so that we may claim the words He spoke of Mary Magdalen : " Many sins are forgiven her, because she hath loved much." [3] It is a happy soul which can weekly in the confessional renew its moral virginity.

To sum up :

1. Regular confession, with the intention of glorifying God, of pleasing Jesus Christ and growing to resemble Him more.

2. Examination of conscience : recapitulation, in the light of love, of the particular and general examinations made during the week.

3. Contrition : to make our own the sentiments of Christ in Gethsemani when He looked upon the sins of the world. Sorrow for having offended Him and stained the image of Christ in our souls.

4. Firm purpose of amendment : the resolution to avoid all sin and all voluntary imperfections for the future, for the love of Christ and through the desire to imitate Him.

---

[2] Luke v, 12, 13.
[3] Luke vii, 47.

5. Prayer to Christ crucified and our Lady of Dolours to obtain the grace to make a confession out of love.

★   ★   ★   ★   ★   ★   ★

This is not the place to go over at length the importance of the spiritual exercises, but there is nothing more effective for shaking off torpor, reviving generosity, renewing the sacerdotal spirit, and sending the soul along the narrow path of perfection. The annual retreat which is required of all religious and priests, and is becoming a regular practice among devout laity, is pre-eminent in its place among these exercises. It is a time of exceptional graces, which should be exploited to the utmost if we are not to show that after all we are but trivial and mediocre in our efforts. If we are to be lukewarm during a retreat it would require something of a miracle to acquire any fervour afterwards. The spiritual exercises are at all times a work of reparation, of sanctification, of preparation. In every single life, no matter how saintly it may be, there are many failings and omissions. It is necessary, then, to be on the watch, strengthening the weak and consolidating the wavering virtues. Sanctification, which is the work of every day and all days, is especially the work of these days of solitude where face to face with our Ideal and more than ever in contact with God, we may sense, a little sadly perhaps, the nostalgia of perfection and the need by our resolutions to make secure the future and our eternity.

This intensive and mighty task of self-sanctification was not embarked upon without a knowledge of self, which in its turn was the result of a profound and detailed examination of the soul and of its life. It is good, then, from time to time to inspect the house as it were from attic to cellar, and to note what is in need of cleaning, repair or improvement. So, the retreat implies a further examination of conscience.

Since our spiritual life is concentrated in the reproduction of Jesus Christ, the imitator of Christ on retreat will make a thorough and stern examination of the progress of his imitation, which will take for its criterion the four great laws of our method and their corresponding procedures.

Contemplation : Have I made Jesus Christ the beginning, middle and end of my spiritual life ? Mass, Communion, prayer, Office, Way of the Cross, Rosary ; recollection, practice of the presence of God, ejaculatory prayers ; studies ; have all these been orientated towards Christ and filled with thoughts of Him, love of Him and interior imitation of Him ? Do we turn continuously towards Christ, like a flower to the sun, in order to live as He lives ?

Prayer : Are we faithful to our prayers, the obligatory ones and those of tradition and supererogation ? Is supplication for graces an integral and essential part of our pious exercises ? Is our devotion to Jesus Christ, to the Holy Ghost, and to the Blessed Virgin, above all the devotion of the suppliant and loving child ? Do our requests have for their principal, if not unique, object the graces of imitation and of resemblance to the Saviour ?

Activity : Is our entire life, in its major outlines and in its minor details, a perfect reproduction of Jesus Christ ? Is imitation of Him the main and exclusive motive power of our whole existence ? Have we, like the Redeemer, made absolute conformity to the will of the Father the immutable programme of our sanctification ? How does our purity of conscience stand ? And obedience to superiors ? The accomplishment of the duties of our state ? Our docility towards grace ?

In all our apostolic works, domestic occupations, deeds and sufferings have we all the time in view, without egotistic introspection, only the glory of the Father and the salvation of souls ? Are we careful to keep this divine intention, which was Christ's, always in its original purity and fervour and to renew it often, perhaps every hour ?

How are we progressing with the practice of the monthly virtue ? At the commencement of each month have we formed the habit of committing to writing precise and earnest resolutions ? Are we vigorous and faithful in keeping them ?

Control : Particular examination : Is this ever voluntarily omitted ? Has it been made on the virtue of the month ? Has it been made in the form of a spiritual confession ?

The Sacrament of Penance : Do we go regularly to Confession ? Every week ? Is it an improvised and rapid confession ? Is it carefully prepared ? Is it a confession made in love and for the glory of God ? Is it conceived as an exercise of imitation of Christ in His attitude towards sin ?

If we submit our imitation of Christ to this careful, thorough and regular check it will escape the danger of any halt or stoppage in its progress, and it will most assuredly repay us with a magnificent reward.

CHAPTER 27

"TASTE AND SEE"

THIS chapter which is a final survey is not intended as an advertisement for the ideas above expressed, but very simply as a justification for the method we have proposed. To judge its value we ought to look at it from both a doctrinal and a practical point of view. Doctrinally it is a method of sanctification which carries, latently at least, scriptural, theological and ascetical teaching ; practically it offers order and method for living the spiritual life. No one denies that the imitation of Christ is an evangelical doctrine. The reproduction of the life of Jesus in ourselves constitutes, as we have stated, the basis and quintessence of Christianity. The debate indeed is not on the subject of imitation, but as to what is the best method of achieving it. It is obvious that the method should be in harmony with the spirit of the Gospel, with the facts of theology and with the principles of asceticism.

Our method is christocentric. It is also theocentric. The Holy Trinity enters the soul and permeates the whole life of the imitator, and each of the Three Persons, Father, Son and Holy Ghost, takes up His abode there and plays His special rôle.

The Father. Our method has oriented our entire existence towards Him, and towards our supreme end. The glory of the Father is all that we desire, work and suffer for, realising literally the exhortation of Saint Paul : " Whether you eat or drink, or what ever else you do, do all to the glory of God."[1] The consciousness of the paternity of God stirs in us the thought of our divine " kinship " and prompts our desire to be true children of the Father. To be the child of God, to enter into the little way of spiritual childhood, to be the brother of Jesus and to resemble Him as brothers do, is the very synthesis of the whole of the spiritual life, and the essence of sanctity.

[1] I Cor. x, 31.

After the Father comes the *Son*. By our method of imitation, Jesus appears in His true perspective as the cornerstone of the building, the keystone of the arch. It is on Him and in Him and through Him that we are building the edifice of our perfection. In His own words He is the Way, the Truth and the Life. The Truth, an ideal to contemplate and to love : the Way which we must take if we wish to imitate Him, and which will lead us to the Father : the Life, for it is in following Christ that we find divine life here on earth while waiting for eternity.

The Holy Ghost in His turn must not be overlooked. Let us see that we ask Him many times during the day to come and form Christ in our souls.

Our method is pre-eminently theological and religious, since we maintain continuous contact with the Holy Trinity. It has, too, a certain relationship with the " christological " doctrine of Saint Paul. The imitation which he preached and practised, " be ye followers of me, as I also am of Christ," was above all the reproduction of the interior life of Jesus and the assimilation of His soul, His qualities, His feelings, much more than a mere repetition of His actions or movements. This is a teaching which is realised in our general procedure of imitation : that is, the general imitation of the Redeemer through conformity with the will of God and the permanent desire to glorify the Father and save souls.

In the matter of asceticism, too, our method, and this is the secret of its power and effectiveness, has the advantage of being able to mobilise and use all the great forces of sanctification. Two beings and two movers concur in the development of our moral life : God and man, grace and our own wills. All supernatural activity is conditioned by divine penetration and the degree of our co-operation with it. The more God acts in us and upon us, and the more readily we give ourselves actively and passively to His quickening and inspiration, so much the more do we approach perfection.

Accordingly the four chief laws and procedures of the imitation of Jesus our Model have for their only aim the ensuring of the powerful, constant and concomitant intervention of grace and goodwill : of grace through contemplation and prayer and of our goodwill through resolutions and control. We truly believe that anyone who adopts this method of imitation as the programme of his life and the instrument of his self-sanctification will have no cause to regret it.

The imitation of Jesus Christ is more too than a doctrine. It is an instrument of salvation both useful and simple to handle. Certain spiritual ways of life, like certain forms of prayer possess a kind of aristocratic and somewhat remote allure, and appear to be purely the heritage of the élite. Our method, on the other hand, though very far from being trivial or commonplace, does appear to be easier of approach, for the simple reason that it possesses two excellent qualities, simplicity and adaptability.

Simplicity is something that we must above all strive for in our spiritual life. Simplicity is to sanctity what the synthesis is to logic or science. One commences with analysis and finishes with the synthesis. What makes a saint is not so much the number and variety of his exterior acts of virtue, as the simplicity and intensity of his interior life, which is entirely composed of faith and love. Similarly, our method of imitation which is in fact the work of our sanctification too, is simplicity itself. It is simple in that it centralises and unifies all the elements of our Christian, religious and priestly life. It is simple in that it sets one precise and unique purpose for all our efforts.

There are no complications about our method, because apart from a few small and entirely optional pious practices, there is no extra burden, no addition whatsoever to our customary round of recollection, prayer and work. Far indeed from being an extra or adventitious devotion, the imitation of Christ integrates perfectly with our life, of which it eventually becomes the framework, or better still, the essence. Nothing is added, but all is restored in Christ. The method has indeed its laws and its customs, but these— contemplation, prayer, action and control—are the fundamental laws of all spirituality. Nothing is included then but what has already been tried and tested by experts in holiness.

Unity which is the cardinal principle of simplicity and the source of sanctity is the keynote of our system. By its means we bring together all our interior and exterior

activity in one unique centre, which is Christ. It was Saint
Thomas who said that God is the principle of unification and
centralisation. To imitate Christ is to centralise all the activities
of our lives around Him, so that in reality we then exist only
through working with Christ. We are no longer an aggre-
gation of disparate elements, remarkable possibly even for
our very differences and eccentricities. Our lives are all united
into one major work, composed of many parts, it is true, but
possessing one basis and one purpose, which consists at all
times and in all things in imitating Christ. The monk, it has
been said, is the man of unity. We have found that unity in
a method of perfect imitation of Christ.

Our life is completely and immutably orientated towards
God. We neither see nor love nor wish anything but the one
thing all the time, to give to all our acts the most sublime
purpose of all, the glory of God through the salvation of the
world. There is nothing left in our existence which veers
towards any other end but this, unique and supreme. Sublime
simplicity, sublime unity.

The second characteristic of our imitation is its suppleness
and adaptability. It allows for the multiplicity of spiritual
temperaments, the variety of states of soul, the infinite differences of circumstances, time, place and personality. Everyone, irrespective of his or her private or public position, age,
occupation or moral dispositions, can without being bent or
broken enter its mould. Everyone can meditate on Jesus
Christ ; can think often upon Him without too much difficulty in the middle of daily occupations ; can pray to Him
and to the Blessed Virgin ; and can, like Him, do the Divine
Will for the glory of God and the salvation of souls. All
this is within the scope of anyone. That the atmosphere of
a monastery or a convent can assist the achievement of this
imitation cannot be denied, but it would be a grave mistake
to consider that our method is incompatible with an intense
and active apostolate. In fact, the contrary is the truth, for
the apostolic life would appear to require it as the very foundation of its safety and its fruitfulness. Whether a man is a
missionary, a parish priest, a curate, or a lecturer and writer,
he still says his prayers, celebrates his Mass, responds to grace,
says his Breviary, recites the Rosary, visits the Blessed

Sacrament, lives in the presence of God and remains faithful
to his practice of recollection. Clearly then, since he formed
the habit in the early years of his religious or sacerdotal life
of returning to Christ and following all these exercises in order
to love Him, to contemplate Him and to reproduce Him in
his own interior life, he can and should carry it into his later
years.

Whether the rector of a parish or of a house of studies,
whether giving missions or retreats, preaching or hearing
confessions, one can give oneself over to all these many works
of zeal, and can fulfil the duties, however humble, of one's
state with the habitual disposition of doing in all of it, like
Jesus Christ, the will of God. It is a very simple matter,
and the very holiness of our ministry should remind us of it,
to renew often our good intentions to look, like our Redeemer,
only for the glory of the Father and the salvation of sinners.
With regard to the virtue of the month, no one will seriously
contend that it is impossible for the fervent soul to make and
keep certain precise resolutions adapted to her needs and in
keeping with her daily life. There is no difficulty either in
sending a constant stream of supplication to Christ, the Holy
Ghost and the Blessed Virgin to obtain all the graces of
imitation. The law of control is the very one which every
priest can and every religious should meticulously observe,
since it involves daily examination, weekly Confession and
the annual retreat.

Moreover, our method is so adaptable that every soul in
no matter what stage of spiritual development can use it
without difficulty. The soul which is starting out on the
spiritual life, the soul which has made good progress, and
even the soul which has attained to perfection can each make
use of it, with more or less success, but never, we believe,
without genuine results.

Finally our method has the merit of ensuring that we shall
come to resemble Jesus Christ in the four ways outlined at
the beginning of our exposition. We shall resemble Him explicitly in that our interior life will be full of the thought
and the love of Him. Many times during the day we shall
turn towards Him to renew in formal terms our resolution
to grow more like Him. We shall identify ourselves, too,

with the transcendentalism of His mission. Thanks to our habit of conformity to the will of God, and to our good intention frequently and faithfully renewed, we shall enter into the same interior dispositions as Jesus Christ, and our lives, like His, will be nothing but a pure hymn of glory to the Father, and a work of redemption.

Then our resolutions formed carefully on the virtue of the month, and faithfully kept and re-examined, will give to our labours the joy of achieving a specific resemblance to the different characteristics of Jesus our Model. Lastly, it will be clear to all that the constant conformity to and exclusive quest for the will of God, with all the exterior and interior renunciations exigent upon it will certainly stamp our work of imitation with the supreme seal of identity with Christ, namely its sacrificial character. So also Mass, Communion, prayer on the Passion and the Way of the Cross, in their turn have helped us to absorb ourselves in the spirit of Christ crucified.

And now, we should like to end with the expression of a wish which will also be our prayer. To all who have read these humble pages with good intentions may our Lord and our Blessed Lady give the grace of knowing, loving and imitating the Saviour more and more until they say, one day, with the Apostle, " I live, now not I, but Christ liveth in me."

★　　★　　★　　★　　★　　★　　★